THE HOWL OF THE MALEMUTE

THE HOWL OF
THE MALEMUTE:

The Story of an Alaskan Winter

———◆———

by SARA MACHETANZ

Photographs by
Fred Machetanz

WILLIAM SLOANE ASSOCIATES
New York   1961

Third Printing , March 1962

Copyright © 1961 by Sara Machetanz
All rights reserved.
Published simultaneously in the Dominion of
Canada by George J. McLeod Limited, Toronto.
Printed in the United States of America.

Library of Congress Catalog Card Number 61–8793

To Cousin Christine

PROLOGUE

Our adventure, like every adventure, had to be one of two kinds—the kind that comes unlooked for, or the kind brought on by one's self.

We brought ours on, by the expending of time and money and by the expending of ourselves on research over a period of years.

All this we did because we knew it needed doing before we would be ready, yet what turned out to be the most important preparation was quite accidental and unpremeditated. These were the years of our lives that prepared *us* for our adventure which took place over an entire winter in sub-arctic Alaska. Obviously, the pivotal event of those years was our going to Alaska.

Fred went first.

He went the year he finished college and twenty years before our adventure became a reality. He was invited by an uncle who had gone to Alaska during the gold rush.

Pioneer Alaskan, Uncle Charlie Traeger, had not discovered gold. He had, instead, spent the last fifty of his eighty years running a trading post in the Eskimo village of Unalakleet.

It was to this village Fred went—flying in a chartered, single-engined plane which landed on the tundra, since there was no air strip in those days. It was from this village he returned not in the six weeks for which he had been invited, but two years later. During that time he had become completely captivated by the colorful life of the Eskimo people and, being an artist, he had found leaving such fascinating subject matter increasingly difficult.

When he did finally bring his extended visit to an end and leave for the "outside," it was with a sea chest bulging with sketches and color notes and a firm determination to go back as soon as possible to what was now his legal residence.

The quickest way to carry out this determination, Fred decided, was to convert his wealth of subject matter into cash through the medium of illustrations. But finding books on Alaska that needed illustrating wasn't as easy as he had thought it would be. His first commission was to illustrate a book dealing with skyscrapers, because the editor liked his use of darks and lights. A few miscellaneous commissions followed and then they were done and there were no more forthcoming, certainly none dealing with Alaska. One editor at last suggested to Fred that the best way to get an Alaskan book to illustrate was to write one himself, so—that was what he did. He wrote not one, but two books—children's books on the Eskimos and their sled dogs and both so lavishly illustrated, even the artist was satisfied.

With the first royalties from the books, Fred returned to Alaska to board a coast guard cutter which visited Eskimo villages all along the west coast as far north as Point Barrow. Again he lost his heart to the friendly, intelligent Eskimos and before the cruise was out, determined to make documenting them his career.

War came and the newly launched career had to be put aside but when Fred volunteered, it was for Alaskan duty. The Aleutian Islands were an area of Alaska he did not know and he wanted to learn all he could about his adopted land. Contrary to much wartime assigning, Fred was given exactly what he asked for. Perhaps the Navy was less than besieged with requests for duty in that remote, fog-shrouded area; perhaps not, but in any case, off he went for three years as an officer in Naval Intelligence.

Meanwhile, though he had no reason for knowing, I, a Tennessean, a one time schoolteacher turned writer, was looking to the day when I could go to Alaska. I took a year's leave of absence from my position with a large Eastern corporation and left for Juneau, Alaska.

Fred, just discharged from the Navy, was back in Alaska to complete his film documentary on the Eskimos. On his way, he stopped in Juneau.

There was a book shop in Juneau, too.

I dropped in there one day, after climbing one of the mountains that rose directly behind the capital city. Wanting to climb that mountain was not surprising for a schoolteacher turned writer who had grown up in the mountains of East Tennessee. It was also not surprising that I mentioned my hike to the bookshop keeper whose reaction, however, was surprising to me, a newcomer: an immediate, vehement reproof.

"You shouldn't have done that, you know. Mountains in Alaska are not like the mountains in Tennessee. They are steep and dangerous. There are bears, killer bears. Every year, someone gets bitten or mauled and then search parties have to be organized and it costs everyone a lot of time and money and worry. *Don't ever go hiking in the mountains alone again up here.*"

Fred looked up from autographing some of his books and

(as he later told me) thought, "I wish I knew her. I'd see she didn't climb the mountains alone again." But I had hurried out, ashamed to appear so unthinking before the distinctive author signing books in the corner.

It was the next day.

Fred was aboard a small mail boat making the run between Juneau and Skagway. I saw him look past the friendly tourist claiming his attention, across the galley and directly at me, the hiker he had seen in the book shop. I felt he wished to be introduced, but there was no chance for that. All the passengers of the boat were crowded in between us. Fred's companion must have been surprised when he suddenly announced in a voice loud enough for everyone to hear that Old Ma Pullen's House was the place to stay in Skagway.

We met on the steps of the Pullen House.

Fred was coming out the door just as I started up the walk and asked if he could help with my bags.

"Yes," I told him and added, "lucky you happened to be here," for there were no bell boys to carry luggage up stairs and down long corridors.

"Yes," he replied and did not add he had been waiting during the two hours I had stayed aboard the boat having lunch with the captain and his crew.

We went on a photographing hike that afternoon and Fred taught me how to handle his press camera.

It took us six weeks to become engaged. Certainly not any longer, with the courtship beginning in historic Skagway, continuing over the gold rush trail to the Klondike, first by scenic narrow-gauge railway, then by stern-wheeler down the mighty Yukon. There were the gold fields of the interior and scenery along the highways to be photographed and now to the fun of being on the same tour was added the interest of an article we were working on together.

The tour ended in Matanuska Valley, but not the romance.

Fred left by plane for Unalakleet, to be assured by Uncle Charlie that two persons would be as welcome at the trading post that winter as one.

In the first month of the New Year there were two, following a wedding in the village mission and a honeymoon by dog team.

Since Fred's project that year was a documentary film of life in an Eskimo village from freeze-up in fall until the break-up in spring, and since I worked with him, I soon began to share the respect and warm regard for the Eskimos held by my new husband. I felt the same reluctance he did when the time came to leave Unalakleet and Alaska for lecture tours with the movie. And the same eagerness to return to Alaska, after each season ended, for more filming, more writing, more painting, and to search out a location for a home.

We found what we were looking for in the Matanuska Valley. Here, to us, was the most appealing scenery in all Alaska. We selected the view we liked the best, centered it in a picture window and built a log cabin around the window. The fact that it happened to be in the heart of three thousand acres of forest was surplus good fortune, as was the fact that it overlooked a perfect blue lake.

There was still another incident that upped our fortunes from merely good to that of extraordinary.

While looking for our homesite, we had bogged down on an unfrequented narrow lane. We had hiked to the nearest farm for help and had come away not only with a farmer on a tractor but with a handsome white sled-dog puppy.

Neither Fred nor I had known we wanted a dog until we saw this one leaping straight into the air and howling to go with us. Suddenly we had wondered what the fun was, living in a tent (which we were doing while building our home) without a dog? What wasted adventure to walk through the forests when there was no eager puppy to lead the way with his nose. How much more reason for hiking down to the lake with a sled puppy who thought he was a retriever and proudly fetched sticks thrown into the water.

We called the puppy Seegoo because that was the Eskimo word for ice and December first—a time of ice—was his birthday.

The cabin was finished as winter set in and we took possession. And Seegoo? He took possession of the high ridge upon which the cabin sat, for he was now a gangling adolescent with heroic ideas of protecting his master and mistress from the porcupines and announcing in loud, clear barks when moose and bear were about, so his master and mistress could protect him if they wanted to.

Seegoo was ever faithful.

When his master and mistress found it necessary to leave he always watched the spot they had last been seen, until they returned.

Seegoo was gentle.

From humans he wanted only affection, nor did he pleasure in fighting his own kind. Were he attacked, he would fight, but mostly he was happy trying to please—both humans and dogs.

Seegoo was adaptable.

When the lecture tours came around, he would walk across lobbies and into elevators with as much aplomb as if he were on the snow carpeted floor of a spruce forest. He appeared on television and on the lecture platform and instead of becoming spoiled, he accepted the adulation of his audiences with kindly dignity. In one month he would total as many miles of travel by auto as other sled-dogs would average in a life time on trail.

In his second year, Seegoo proved himself "under duress."

That was on an expedition to photograph a lake which annually broke its dam of glacier ice and disappeared. It was a trip requiring ruggedness, from the landing of the Seabee on a lake glutted with icebergs to a crash on taking off some three weeks later. During the stay at the lake, we had some fifty miles of packing to do—and Seegoo, too—wearing saddlebags. The way lay over forty-five degree slopes of sharp talus—so sharp, it cut through hard rubber soled boots and through the tough pads of sled dogs. There were alders to be crawled under and through and when Seegoo's saddlebags hung up, did he use that as an excuse to rest or give up? No indeed. He backed up and tried again and again until he could get through. There were deep, swift cascades treacherous for any dog, but especially for a sled dog meant to travel on snow and ice.

After one stretch of particularly punishing terrain, Fred lay on his side on a steep incline to take a break. He looked at Seegoo, lying on his belly flanked by bulky packs. Seegoo, panting in the hot sun, paws bleeding, muscles aching, looked up, eyes soft with devotion, wagged his tail, ready to go at his master's word.

"Sled dogs are such magnificent creatures," Fred said. "We should make a movie glorifying them, Sara."

I was immediately responsive. Besides sounding like a challenging project, the discussion ought to be good for several more minutes of rest. I mentioned they were much maligned in stories of the gold rush days and Fred declared such a movie as he had in mind would be completely authentic. From there on our interest took fire.

Such a job had never been done.

It *should* be done—the life of a sled dog from the time he was born until he ran in a team.

Sled dogs were a vital component of the Alaskan scene,

but as working dogs they were rapidly becoming extinct. They must be documented before this happened.

It would take time.

The locale was fore-ordained—Unalakleet. There were many reasons why. Even though Uncle Charlie had passed away and the trading post had changed hands, the Eskimos there were our friends and the surroundings familiar. We even knew the dogs in the village. There were lovely spruce forests nearby—a scenic advantage over the majority of Eskimo villages strung along the bleak northwestern coast of Alaska.

Equipment had to be compiled—a special sleeping bag made to order for camping out in sub-zero temperatures, tents, portable heaters, lamps and clothing were a few of the more important items.

There must be a preliminary trip to make arrangements for a place to live and for a team and actors. There must even be a preliminary litter of puppies so we would know what stages of development to expect.

Finally, after three years of concentrating on getting ready, all of these things had been done.

A cabin was waiting at Unalakleet. A team was waiting. Mrs. Seegoo had been shipped over by air several weeks before due to her "delicate condition." Groceries and a ton and a half of dog food for the year were on order.

The day came—a fine fall day.

Seegoo entered his crate at the airport terminal in Anchorage without hesitation. He knew this meant some kind of exciting change.

The plane was boarded, engines were revved and with a roar we headed down the runway and were airborne.

The direction was north, north west.

Our adventure had begun.

THE HOWL OF THE MALEMUTE

CHAPTER

1

Over the high grass waving outside the window, I saw Fred straighten up and start towards our sod-banked cabin.

"Will you come out here a minute?" he asked as he opened the door and, before I could answer, turned and was gone.

I hurried after him: into the crispness of September by the Bering Sea; past our pet malemute, Seegoo, whose tail suddenly came alive; around and between our four other sled dogs to a large dog house with a wide door, a puppy house, which in this instance was serving as a delivery room.

We dropped to our knees before the opening.

"How many are there now?" I whispered.

"Seven," was the reply, "and I can't believe it but I think they're all females. I want you to look. Maybe I'm wrong."

I reached over and stroked the mother, Geena. Gently, with the other hand, I picked the squirming lumps out of the straw. When I had finished, there was no doubt. They were all females. We sat back on our heels and looked at each other.

We were to document these puppies in color cinemascope movies, a project with three year's research and preparation behind it. Yet with all our planning the possibility of an all female litter had never occurred to us. Our shooting script had been drawn up on a sire-son relationship climaxing in the puppy team on the floating ice of spring. By that time any one of this litter of females might enter a breeding period. It would be impossible to run them, still we would have to end the movies with the same puppies we had used in the beginning.

"Maybe there'll be more."

Fred shook his head. "I doubt it. It's been some time since the last."

"What are we going to do?"

"Do? Why, take movies of them. That's what we're here for."

He strode to the door of our outer room and with an automatic genuflect to keep from bumping his head, disappeared inside. When he came out, he was carrying not our usual large tripod but a very short one, one that would record impressions from a puppy's eye level.

We "set up" directly in front of the puppy barn.

Geena was oblivious to the photography as she licked and nursed her puppies. She was an all-over silver-grey malemute, except for a faint mask which gave her a quizzical expression. Today, however, her face showed only tenderness and the picture of her and the puppies was one of deep basic appeal. So appealing we forgot our lunch and when we did remember, hurried our eating to return and look.

It was then I saw Fred's mouth form a soundless oh.

"There are nine puppies," he exclaimed. "Nine!"

Now, one at a time, Fred counted them off again and on the fourth, "This one's a male," he cried. And on the seventh, "Here's another one—another male!"

Then more puppies had been born. Sons for Seegoo—fat worms, wrinkled, sightless, flailing the palm of Fred's hand —and with them our chances for success in our project increased by two.

Pleasant as it was to watch the newborn, we couldn't spend the afternoon that way. There were other phases of the project to be taken care of. The first involved Jacob Soxie, one of the two men living in Unalakleet who still made sleds. This he did and did well between loading and unloading planes for the airline servicing the village.

We started down our path, a trough in grass already warned by the first frosts of winter. And over to a wider path which served as a road to an air field on the tundra in summer and a main route for dog teams in winter.

Throughout the village, the Eskimos were breaking the crusts on their gardens, gathering the last vegetables for storage in their cellars. Everywhere were sounds of getting ready for winter; repairing and chinking log cabins, the pounding of axes against steel as oil drums were made into dog houses or incinerators or containers for ice and water. And there was the continuous sawing of logs towed down from spruce forests several miles up the Unalakleet River.

We met two village matrons wearing knapsacks, the one carrying a large birch bucket, the other a .22 rifle. They were going to hunt ptarmigan and gather berries, blueberries and cranberries, though they did not expect to find many of the latter. "Too much rain. We miss them this winter." We sympathized, knowing the cranberries which grew low on the ground and had the taste of Swedish lingonberries were a welcome addition to the winter diet of fish, seal and canned goods.

"We glad you couples is back," they told us, and were on their way.

"There's that old rascal again!" Fred shouted affectionately at the approach of an Eskimo, silver-haired, eyes smiled almost shut. This was standard greeting for Dave Paniptchuk who acted as interpreter at mission services and was an authority on many things, including sled dogs.

"Hello, Fred. Hello, Missis. We glad you couples is back."

"Hello," Fred rejoined. Then, because he knew of Dave's interest in dogs, "Our female had pups today. Nine of them."

Dave's brows bounced up. "Yah?"

"Yes. Two males and seven females."

"Seven females! That's a shame."

"Oh, they'll be all right for movies, I guess."

"You make movies?"

"Yes, of these puppies. From the time they're born until they run as a team."

"A movie of *dogs*?"

"Yes."

There was a pause. To Dave this was inexplicable. He walked along with us. "I get three whales this summer."

"Good for you." Dave was one of a decreasing number of hunters who still went for "belugas" each year.

"I think I get killer whale in my net. It tored the net and get away but it leave a little muk-tuk (skin) so I know. I sold a whole stomach full of blubber to the Indians at Kaltag. They paid me 35 cents a pound. They're crazy for it."

We congratulated him.

"Maybe I get another. I'm still camping across the river but I come see the puppies when I'm back," he promised us, turning off to his son's home.

Jacob, we were told when we arrived at his cabin, was down at the slough. We followed a path between his cache, hung with traps and harnesses, and his sled dogs; past a fish rack strung with salmon; to the top of a steep bank where a net drying in the sun checkered the blue sky beyond. And down the bank to the river slough running parallel to the Bering Sea and forming the spit which was Unalakleet. There we found Jacob working on an outboard motor.

"Our female had nine pups today," Fred announced as we came up.

"Yah?"

"Seven females."

Jake stopped his work. "What you do? Kill 'em?"

"We can't. We have to make movies of them."

"Movie of *dogs?*"

"Yes."

Jake shook his head.

"There's nothing else we can do. We want you to make a sled for them."

"O.K." this Jake understood.

He would attend to getting the wood—oak imported from "outside"—at one of the two village trading posts. He would also buy the other essentials: screws and braces and thong, or romaine as it was called, for lashing.

"We'll want to take movies of you making the sled," Fred told him. "When do you think you will start on it?"

Jake shrugged. "I go upriver. Get wood first."

"A couple of weeks?"

Jake was silent, figuring. "Before the first snow," he announced.

How he knew when the first snow of winter would fall was a mystery to us but, with no more assurance than that, we had to leave the matter.

Back on the main path, children ran and played on their way home from school. Their fur parkas and boots incongruously combined with mail-order clothing was evidence of the change in the traditional dress.

"Hello, Missis, Hello, Barney," they greeted us, the latter because they were reading one of our books at school and chose to associate Fred with the hero. For the same reason, they were more than ordinarily interested in See-goo, another leading character. Daily they would come to pet him and marvel at his abnormally large size. We had been surprised. Sled dogs were generally regarded by the villagers as no more than work animals but to the children, Seegoo had become a lovable personality through read-ing about him.

They trotted along beside us now and when they caught sight of Seegoo exclaimed excitedly, "There's Beeg Dog!"

Long before they saw him, "Beeg Dog" knew we were coming, having heard our voices.

From the moment we left, Seegoo always watched the place he had seen us last until we returned. As we came into view, his ears folded flat against his head. There was no other sign of recognition. With legs crossed, he lay still on top of his house, for dignity was as much a part of our 100-pound pet as was his polar bear coloring and size.

Once he was certain we were coming, however, he dove to the ground, tried once to check himself in a stretch which lost any effect of indifference as it ended in a joyous howl and frantic thrashing of the tail. This was the cue for our other dogs to join in. Not having been worked since the spring before, they were looking for the slightest excuse to break their boredom.

Though Seegoo led the chorus, he was the neophyte of the team, never having known time in harness. Other than a short stint of packing his entire travel experience had been by auto or air, yet we had decided he must be our leader be-cause he was the most handsome sled dog we had seen any-where. Due to his looks, Seegoo commanded attention wherever we went. He was used to accepting it though he never condescended to beg for it; even now, when he had to share court with his offspring, for Geena's house soon proved a Mecca to the children.

We did not have to caution them against handling the puppies. From infancy, they had been taught not to go near a nursing mother dog. Instead, they would stop several paces away to bend low and peer at the puppy-house door and then run off to spread the news.

How quickly news traveled, we realized after the children's first visit. Within a few minutes, our near neighbor and friend, Elizabeth Sarren, came over.

"Johnny brought news," she referred to her four-year-old adopted son. "He say you been got pups."

"That's right." We went over to look at them.

"Nine," Fred told her. "Two males and seven females."

"Ee-nee-gee!" (not good)

"Oh, it won't make any difference in the movies."

"Females lotsa trouble," she disagreed.

We decided to go for fresh straw not only for the puppy house but for the other dogs too.

"I go with you. I help," Elizabeth volunteered. "It take lotsa grass. Straw dogs lie on turn to ice in cold weather. Have to put new straw in then. Better to get before snow."

We walked to the stretch of tundra between our cabin and the Bering Sea. As we worked, Elizabeth displayed an efficiency developed through generations of gathering grass. Stiff-legged, she leaned over to pull a handful close to the ground and without straightening up, tucked it in her lap. In this manner she could handle a large quantity and at the same time have use of both hands.

She held up a different kind of grass—not coarse or large around.

"This for boots. Put inside, keep warm, dry. It not crush quick as dog grass."

"Maybe I should gather some of that, too?"

Elizabeth shook her head. "Grass from creek up in hills better. It not have salt air. Stay dry longer. Get in spring, good only little time. I just get. Good for long time. I have lots to give you." She took the large bunch from her lap and tied it into a bundle with strands of grass knotted together. "I go now." She started off, then half turned. "Maybe females all right—for movie pictures."

Fred and I continued working until there were several bundles and then we went to bed our dogs.

First there was Geena and the pups. The new mother did not get up until we thrust a bundle beside her. Then, gratefully she moved over, nosing the pups out of the straw to her teats.

When we went to Seegoo, he proceeded unhurriedly out of his house, stood and watched us make his bed and re-entered just as deliberately as if the straw was placed by his order. He had always been extraordinarily adaptable.

Next we went to the sled dog, Lynx. It was difficult to get to his house for he was out and all over us, jumping up, licking our hands and faces. He was called Lynx because of his coloring, but had we done the naming, it would have been "Coon" since his face was exactly like that of a raccoon. He was fat and lazy, so we had been told by the Eskimo owner from whom we had leased him. He also had the reputation of being a fighter but we hoped through affection and training to break him of it.

His next door neighbor, Arbo, was as withdrawn as Lynx was outgoing. While we arranged his bed, Arbo sat erectly by his post, the mask over his eyes giving him a slightly worried expression. Even the markings on his coat which resembled a cutaway carried out his air of formality. The word "Arbo" was not native dialect as we had at first supposed but his owner's contraction of the two words "Our

Boy." The owner had been glad to lease Arbo, the dog being six years old and considered past his prime for work. But neither Lynx's laziness nor Arbo's age mattered to us. We were not interested in speed but in a photogenic team and they were both good looking, though quite different in appearance.

When we went to our last two dogs, they were busily engaged in play-fighting; turning, feinting, sprinting, all within the radius of their six-foot chains. They were coated in silver flecked black which gave them a wild wolf look but both were reliably friendly. While Brandy, in his prime at three years, handled himself skillfully, Ot-key-luk, which meant "No Name" and who was just twelve months old, skidded and bounced with the awkwardness of adolescence. Brandy was aesthetically inclined, being one of the star howlers in the village. Ot-key-luk was a born clown. These two we would run at wheel, the hardest position next to the sled, to make up in pulling power what Lynx and Arbo lacked.

This then was our team: Seegoo, the magnificent; Lynx, the lazy; Gentleman Arbo; Singer Brandy and Ot-key-luk, the clown. Upon them would depend our transportation, our getting wood and water and the carrying out of our project—even perhaps our lives. We had taken care of them first. Now it was time to put our own house in order for the winter.

CHAPTER

2

The home we had chosen for this winter was a squat cabin with one ten-by-twelve room and a six foot wide outer room locally referred to as a "porch."

From the ground to the eaves, it was banked with sod blocks except on one wall where a section had fallen away to reveal moss-chinked upright logs. Sheets of corrugated iron with streamers of rust flying from every nail hole covered the log roof. There were two windows, one facing the Bering Sea on the west and one facing the village on the south. The door to the outer room opened south as did the doors on all the cabins in the village. This was due to the almost constant east-west wind which left monstrous snow drifts in winter to point its direction—also a fifteen degree list to our stove pipe.

We had rented it when we had come to Unalakleet the spring before to make arrangements for the present movie project. We had paid $75 for the year and our Eskimo landlord had tried to refund $5 of that because he felt the amount in excess of value.

Our choice of the smallest cabin in the village was beyond

the understanding of our native friends. "Dog House" one of them called it. There was no doubt Fred "lost face" in bringing his wife to such a place, especially with story-and-a-half houses, copied after the quarters at the nearby Federal Aviation Agency Station, available. Still, it happened to be exactly what we wanted. It was picturesque and, more important, authentic. It had, in fact, been built and lived in by Eskimos before its last occupancy by a prospector. It would be easy—much easier—to heat than the larger houses. With its sod-banked walls, it seemed not only substantial but harmonious with the country. We gave it the name "Mik-nik-rok," meaning "the smallest," and moved in.

The interior walls and ceiling of hewn logs were faced with soot-smeared cardboard. Only the shiny, smoke-blackened ridge pole showed through and in the west gable, a fist-sized piece of sky we took to be for purposes of ventilation.

There was a table nailed to the wall under the south window, a bench and two top heavy hand-made stools and a washstand. To this our landlord added an old Yukon stove with a firebox about the size of one shoe box atop another. Missing, however, were the firebricks protecting the tiny oven from the firebox.

Our first acquisition had been a fifty gallon drum for holding water. We realized the limitations of our new home when the drum proved too wide for the door and it had been necessary to remove a window to bring it in. To the drum we had added a plywood cover and a bucket and dipper on top of that. Next, a bed had been rented for the year for $10. It was a single iron cot with the lines of an occupied hammock, but by supplementing the sag with our sleeping bag we made it passably comfortable. There had been difficulty getting this piece of furniture in, too. No wonder—with six small children crowded inside to watch. We had sent them outdoors where they had clustered at the window only to scatter like quail when Fred turned suddenly in their direction. The washstand we had equipped with a basin, the necessary "catch bucket" and a mirror Fred had to crouch to look into because of the low pitch of the roof.

This was the extent of our fixing-up the spring before and this is what we had come back to. Now our task was to make it as comfortable as possible for the long northern winter.

We began by removing the dirty cardboard facing. Then, rather than have it go to waste as very little ever did in this country, we lined the walls of our outer room with it. We had hoped to leave the hand-hewn log interior exposed but after several showers of dried moss and dust following the slightest jar, we gave up the idea. Instead, we ordered tan insulating paper. It came by air from Anchorage five days later—the morning we noticed the puppies' ears had become tiny flaps instead of folds against their heads. It was transported to our door in the airlines pickup driven by an Eskimo employee, who during off-hours ferried trappers to and from the village in his own plane.

In the same delivery was also two thousand pounds of our freight for the year. This was in addition to the ton-and-a-half of dried meal for the dogs, gasoline and crates of groceries which had arrived previously by ship. Such bulk supplies the trader was good enough to store for us at the trading post.

The following week we spent installing, improving and improvising and when we had finished, the only trace of the original interior was the vent hole. We did leave the ridge pole shiny and black because we thought it gave character to the room but with our fixing-up, it sprouted a runner of clothesline down its length for drying socks and the felt insoles of our boots.

The walls and ceiling were completely covered with tan insulating paper which, though cleaner and lighter, gave us the feeling of living inside a grocery bag. To offset this, we brightened the floor with plaid linoleum and painted the window sills, gables and furniture a vibrant red. The washstand and catch bucket were transformed into a washroom with gleaming white paint. We combined red and white in checkered oilcloth for our table and the shelves over the stove.

While many of our trappings were ordered from Anchorage, some were not. Like everyone else in this land of necessarily high prices, we "gleaned."

The handsome sets of shelves that held our staples on one side of the south window and our books and cameras on the other were "gleaned" from the school rubbish heap. Our ten-gallon metal cylinder wastebasket had once held cement. The linoleum covering the top of the washstand and our bench and stools were scraps from recent buildings —either the nurse's clinic or the two-family teacherage.

Though we didn't plan it that way, the outstanding feature of our new decor at Mik-nik-rok was the kerosene lamp. In its warm yellow light was comfort akin to the open hearth. It invited one's hand to the cup and a settling back for unhurried telling of tales. It turned the paper walls to honey and set the red paint glowing. That it gave off magic was proven when Elizabeth called to view the results of our labors and exclaimed, "Why, it look like picture in magazine!"—the ultimate compliment.

Once the interior was comfortable, we started on the outside.

First sod blocks had to be cut from the tundra and banked against our east wall. Luckily we had a stretch of perfect fall weather, energy air-born and blue skies reflecting toward evening a red as from many fires.

While we worked, we caught the first intimation of a howl from the puppy house. Pitched in a shaky treble, it was a marked advance over the mewing, gurgling and squeaking the pups had limited themselves to from birth. Though they still pushed around on their bellies, they would occasionally stand on their hind legs to reach an unused teat.

Fred undertook to construct shelves in the outer room to hold our current supply of gasoline and kerosene, fuel oil, a chain saw, a stock of groceries, extra film, dog food and harnesses. On the walls were hooks for boots and parkas, on the floor a sea chest with linens and, swinging from the ceiling, our snowshoes. Literally, we lived in every layer of space at Mik-nik-rok.

In one corner of the outer room was our solution to one of the most vexing problems of northern living. It was a chemical toilet, a five-gallon oilcan encased in a wooden box with a vent pipe through the roof. We had mail-ordered a toilet seat but what arrived—shell pink and delicately lined—was much too fine for our fundamental setup. So we had regretfully sent it back and "gleaned" a sturdier, home-made affair from the trader. The method of sewage disposal recommended by the Native Service were "sanitary aids," fifty-gallon drums minus the ends, set in the ground and topped with removable lids. Since the spit was sand and gravel, the drainage was good and the system worked well. Our chemical facilities, however, remained unique. Chemical was expensive and usually families were too large to make such a system practicable. A few sanitary aids there were, and fewer outhouses.

The chemical toilet was just one of the many fillings and emptyings that made up our living.

There was the lamp to be filled, the fuel oil container, the water drum, and the wood to be replenished. There were ashes to be emptied, the catch buckets and the garbage and cans. For the garbage and cans we installed a wooden box beneath the Yukon stove. We equipped it with rope handles so it could be slid out and back. Such utilization of otherwise unused space always gave us an outsized sense of pleasure. Just as when we found that the tripods and fresh produce and potatoes would fit exactly under the table. And that wood could be stacked between the stove and the wall.

When our garbage and cans box was filled, the contents were transferred to fifty-gallon drums outside. From there on, it was taken care of by the Unalakleet garbage collection service. Every Saturday the maintainance man at school would make the rounds in a school-owned tractor drawing a crude cart. It was a service set up by the village council, the charge for which was 10 cents per week.

The garbage conveyor was only one of a number of motorized vehicles to appear in the village since Fred had lived here with his trader uncle twenty years before. The dog-team mail delivery of those days had given way to bush pilot service and later, commercial airline service. Now there were trucks and jeeps from the FAA Station and a motor scooter. A few bicycles were to be seen and even a baby stroller. Every mail day, a truck came from a recently established military installation several miles up the coast. All these conveyances had necessitated the building of a road, a wide graveled highway paralleling the sea. The noise from the motors and planes still seemed alien to us, yet without them we would not have had Anchorage papers three times a week nor the groceries which came to us by air: bread which cost 60 cents a loaf, lettuce at 50 cents a pound, and eggs $1.50 per dozen—all plus freight.

We were not alone in ordering by air. A few of the villagers were regular customers, too, and both trading posts enlivened their offering of canned and dried goods with fresh produce, bread and such delicacies as sandwich meats. Unfortunately, air cargo was subject to weather, the freight section of the plane being unheated and produce liable to freeze. Or, in warm weather if the plane was unable to land due to fog or storm, meats might spoil in several days of shuttling back and forth. Still, we made out quite well. There was homemade bread for sale in the village, 50 cents a small loaf, 75 cents a large. And so many of the villagers who came to call brought bread that we had more than we could use.

Among the sharers of bread were the teacher, Lillian Russell; the nurse, Iris Jette; our good neighbor, Elizabeth Sarren; Marian Gonongnan, who considered herself Fred's foster mother; Rod Moore, a young air force man renting the cabin immediately in front of ours, and Martha Nanouk. Martha, who said, "If someone is nice to you, you can pay it back by being nice to their relatives." She was repaying us for kindnesses Fred's late Uncle Charlie had once shown her, not only with bread, but with pans to help us set up housekeeping—so many, our cabin wouldn't hold them all. When we returned the overflow, she pressed a freshly shot ptarmigan on us. Though that might be her last, Martha believed, "When one thing is gone, there is always something else. Nature provides." Martha's daughter had been generous too, bringing towels made from sugar sacks and tender cabbage from her garden. Another neighbor brought us a goose. We felt him entirely too generous and insisted on paying but he was just as insistent that we not. "You ask me for goose, you get to pay for it. I ask you to take it, I get to give it." We did not argue further. Instead, we ordered extra fruits and meats or vegetables from Anchorage. When we took over two heads of lettuce, tomatoes and four bananas to him it was not refused. This way, their diet was varied with foods they would not have otherwise enjoyed and the same was true for us.

This sharing of food, both taking and partaking, led to the popular pastime of calling.

Callers came to Mik-nik-rok from the moment we moved in.

Among the first was our old friend, Thora Katchatag, welcoming us back. Quickly we made room for her on the bench but Thora already sat on the floor, legs outstretched and she would not move, for this she preferred. Straightway a cup of coffee for her and some cookies. Thora was one of the village's busiest midwives. How different was her attending expectant mothers with a kit of essentials prepared under the supervision of the nurse, from the days of her own birth.

As was the custom, Thora's mother had entered a snowbank with the first pains of labor. Except for a lining of grass, there were no comforts and here she was to stay alone and unattended for three days after the birth or "until the infant's navel dried up." Thora showed us how women would kneel with one heel pressed against the rectum to prevent tearing. But she herself had not been born in the snowbank. Someone had walked over it while her mother was inside and "stopped the labor." Upon hearing of the situation, the missionary's wife had hurried over and after some persuasion coaxed her out and into the house. Thus did Thora claim the distinction of being the first baby in the village to be born outside of a snowbank.

"Now it all changed. But sometime womans still go on knees to make baby come."

She was full of the story of delivering a baby aboard ship the summer before. It was on the Coast Guard Cutter *Storis* which made an annual cruise along the Arctic and

Bering Sea Coast to bring medical and dental care to the natives.

"She (the prospective mother) have all her teeth pulled out but that not hurt. She have pain in stomach. It was baby starting. She wake me up in the middle of the night."

"What were you doing on the *Storis* at night?" we wanted to know.

"They get some kind of message during day. Some kind of 'mergency to look for something," Thora explained. "They went to look before anybody get off. The doctor, he in Unalakleet. They leave him. Night come. We all sleep anywhere. Then this woman, she wake me. I go looking for someone. Finally I look down hole in floor. 'What you want?' somebody yell. I say 'Woman's sick. I need help.' He take me to captain. But," Thora cocked her head, "I captain from the start of that woman's labor. Everybody do what I say. 'Get me room.' They get me room. They get room full of guns—"

"The arsenal?"

"Yes. I think that what you call it. 'Get me sheets. Get me rags. I need something tie cord with. Get me box for baby.' I really boss those mens around," she chortled.

The mid-wife was often given the privilege of naming new babies and this time was no exception. Thora promptly called the new born boy "Storis" after the ship.

We asked her how many babies she had delivered now and she told us 163 in the last twelve years.

While she talked three children had come to call. They stood silently and listened. Nor did they even move.

From then on, the children came in couples or up to half a dozen at a time. They came out of curiosity. They came to get warm. Or to look at the bright colors in the room. Their soft tapping might be heard at the door from the time our shades went up in the morning until our lamp went out at night. They would file in and stand grinning, waiting to be asked what they wanted, a question usually answered with, "nothing," or, "oh I just come to see you," or a shake of the head or giggles.

They stood by while we scrubbed our teeth and combed our hair and though we didn't care for an audience, neither did we want to discourage their coming. Two inflexible rules we established. They were not to visit while we were typing or eating and many days these were the only times we had to ourselves.

When not calling on us, they would pay homage to Seegoo or gather in front of the puppy house. With their outsized white cotton gloves which were standard dress for all ages, they looked stiff armed as scarecrows. Still the faces peering out from the fur ruffs were anything but lifeless—snapping black eyes and ruddy cheeks belying the colds, earaches and tuberculosis to which they were subject.

Among the children, one of the boys stood out. He was Howard Sarren, a natural mimic and actor. He had a wonderfully expressive face, a quick and perfect smile and, though thirteen years old, appeared to be much younger. From the start he attached himself to us. He confided he wanted to be a "hillbilly" singer when he grew up and demonstrated his talents all in the same breath, lapsing into a native chant and dance. Immediately we decided here was the boy hero for our sled dog movie. We asked him if he would like to work for us and the answer was an eager "yis." Then, because we wanted him reporting every day in the event there was movie work, we offered him a token job of emptying our wastebasket and burning trash. Howard was overjoyed.

To get better acquainted we had him to supper. It turned into a protracted meal with our young guest taking undersized bites, chewing overlong and rolling the food around and around in his mouth before he could bring himself to the irrecoverable swallow. He particularly liked "better than salmon trout" the pork chops, but all the food he found eminently acceptable. He ate until a button popped off his shirt and after that until he was miserably uncomfortable.

"Howard would rather have a plate of food in front of him than a week's wages," Fred observed later and it was true. Yet the compulsion did not come from having known hunger so much as a hopeless addiction to tasty food.

We engaged another of the children, Sarah Soxie, for domestic help. Seven years before, when we had spent the winter in Unalakleet, Sarah's sister Daisy had been my dishwasher. Now, Sarah seemed glad to carry on the tradition. She was as shy as Howard was outgoing. She would slip through the door, greet us with a duck of the head and go directly to the dishes. Nearly always she brought one or more school chums with her and while she worked, they would sit solemnly looking over the cabin or us.

Not more than a week had gone by when we found a way to break through this reserve. "What's news?" we would ask as Sarah and her friends came through the door.

At first there was just a flirt of pigtails and a giggle. Then, "So and so have birthday." After that, there was a daily report of birthdays in the village. Birthdays were of especial importance to the Eskimos. By young and old, they were observed usually with a party and cake and pudding or hand-cranked ice cream. We wondered how Sarah kept up on the birth dates of so many people until she told us they were announced in school.

Though only twelve years old, Sarah proved to be completely competent. Most important of all, she was "saving of water." The rinse water from one day's dishes was carefully put by for the next day's washing. She always checked if the dish water were needed to scour any of our various catch buckets before she went to "spill it." This near reverence for water had no doubt grown out of years of conserving it in her own home.

We developed a certain frugality, too, after our first trip upriver. There we had dipped water, bucket by bucket, into a fifty-gallon drum but the real work hadn't begun until back at the village. Bucket by bucket the drum had to be emptied into a twenty-gallon corrugated can, pushed by wheel barrow across the quarter-mile spit to our cabin and carried bucket by bucket again to the drum in our cabin.

With freeze-up, the process would become more tedious and time consuming and that freeze-up was near, we were certain. We could hear its approach each morning as our dogs crunched ice crusted overnight in their water pans. Seegoo chose to take his pan inside his house. We didn't know whether this was a maneuver to melt it or whether he was developing a sense of possession, with all the other dogs around him.

Getting wood was just as laborious. Again, the source of supply was several miles upriver. And again, the real work wasn't in the felling, limbing, upending to the river, lashing to the boat and towing, but when it finally arrived at the slough and had to be sawed into sections and transported by wheelbarrow across the spit. Driftwood or "dry" wood, as it was called, brought $3 a sled load and to this had to be added $1.50 for breaking it into stovewood lengths. Split spruce was $2 per bushel basket. To offset this cost of living, there was one solution. Get your own. And that was what we chose to do.

CHAPTER

3

On the first of October—the puppies had begun to look like dogs because their eyes were now open—we went for our winter's supply of wood.

With us was our air force neighbor, Rod Moore. We furnished the motor, boat, food and gasoline at 80 cents a gallon in return for Rod's help and the "knowhow" he had acquired doing log work in Maine. He was also entitled to a share of the logs but since he used an oil-burning stove except when baking, his needs were negligible. Mostly, he went for a chance to work in timber again.

Besides getting a winter's supply of wood, the men were out to do two things. One, to prove that the logs might be rafted downriver almost as quickly as they could be towed, which was the accepted method. What extra time it took, they reasoned, would be more than paid for in the savings of gasoline—a considerable item at 80 cents per gallon. The other, to bring back the largest raft of the fall.

We started from the slough around ten in the morning. Logs and parts of rafts lined its banks yet no one worried about their wood being stolen and, so far as we knew, none ever was. Along the water's edge, women cleaned fish, splitting them lengthwise to be hung and dried. They were the last of the salmon run and quite discolored—a gray or mustard color but "good for dog food," our friends told us. Contrary to usual practice, they did not save the roe because, they told us "not good when beginning to hatch."

As we passed, villagers looked up from their work to wave. They must have wondered why, with out boat low in the water, we chose to take Seegoo. But after five years of his faithful companionship, we never once thought of leaving him behind. He was certainly a picture of canine contentment sitting in the bow of the boat, ears folded flat as if by a mighty wind.

The river was lovely, a dark, clean cut canal coiling through flats of rusty grass. Then came tundra. And after two or three miles, birch and willows letting go their last shreds of brown, and scrub spruce. The river, always difficult to navigate, was even more so now. As feeder streams froze, the water had become shallow and the channel more narrow. The safest procedure was to cut away at the bends and steer towards the banks where the water ran deep. From the undersides of the banks, winter showed its fangs in icicles which remained unmelted in the below-freezing temperature.

We passed several women out to get water and farther up, a boat loaded with three generations of menfolk. It was towing a second boat filled with sled dogs and women packing babies on their backs. Crammed around them were the supplies and equipment they were bringing back from their summer fishing camp.

All the camps along the banks were deserted but fish still hung drying from the racks, a canvas protecting them against the rain. Beside each rack was a frame for a tent and occasionally an aerial for a radio.

Around noon, we saw the beginnings of a raft by the river bank. At the same time, the wood gatherer heard our motor and in a moment a bull-shouldered form emerged from the woods. A hand snatched a knitted cap from a thatch of hair and waved it to and fro. It was Andy Bango, one of the Laplanders whose family had come to Alaska to herd reindeer when they were first brought over from Siberia.

We turned toward the bank and were just starting to secure when Seegoo leaped into the water, over his head. Though Andy coaxed him, Seegoo refused to go ashore without us. Desperately he clawed at the edge of the boat, a touching show of loyalty but a damp one for when we hauled him out, he immediately shook himself and sprayed us with water.

Andy invited us to his tent. It was small and pitched so low we had to crawl to enter. Thus did he conserve the heat from a portable stove made by wiring two five-gallon gasoline tins together. We divided the sandwiches we had brought and Andy boiled coffee in a two-pound coffee can, smoke blackened from use and equipped with wire handles. While we ate he reminisced of camping with the deer; of tents frozen so stiff a stove pipe had to be forced through its opening and a fire built to thaw the fabric in order to put it up. He also gave us a recipe for breakfast: bury a deer head, build a fire over it that would last the night and when you get up in the morning "breakfast ready."

"Are you going to buy any of the North Star reindeer?" we asked our host. This was the topic of the moment at Unalakleet. The last ship of the season, the *North Star*, was due to bring slaughtered reindeer from the herds on the island of Nunivak. Though there was a local herd, the herder seldom had deer to spare and so the villagers were looking forward to this chance of getting some fresh meat.

But Andy would have none of it, he declared. "I like fat deer and every time I get lean." Perhaps he had become highly selective through years of having his pick of a herd.

As we climbed back into our boat to leave, Andy pointed out that we were in danger of being caught upriver by the freeze-up. He had tied his raft in a slough the night before and that morning been forced to cut it out of 20 feet of ice. This added to the urgency we had felt each time we passed a stream already glassed over.

In midafternoon, we turned off at the Siroski River about twenty-five miles from Unalakleet. The river was perhaps the width of four skiffs and swift running. It was so tortuous that in several places it had cut across narrow portages to leave strangulated loops of stagnant water. The bordering forests were heavily wooded, showing little evidence of logging.

We selected a high bank with a thick grove of spruce and alder, good protection against wind and storms, and the men began to make camp. Though the sky was the characteristic greenish-yellow preceding night, it was quite dark in the forest and necessary to light the gasoline lantern so they could see to clear, cut sapling for tent poles and drive in stakes. No sooner was our camp set up, than we realized we had borrowed a tent literally as large as Mik-nik-rok. The space it afforded was entirely out of proportion to our sources of heat, a gasoline cooking stove and a kerosene burner yet to be tested. There was nothing to do but make it smaller.

So, while I prepared supper beneath, the men lowered it the height of the side walls and dropped the back to make a lean to. Still it was uncomfortably cold.

The kerosene heater, though functional in appearance and in the advertised word, did not work out in practice. It would not warm an area larger than the palm of one's hand and that only at a distance of about six inches. We dubbed it the "Little Failure" but kept it burning until we retired for the psychological warmth it gave. After that first night, when we awoke to a lid of ice in our water bucket and the felt insoles of our boots frozen stiff, we resorted to a less modern but more comforting wood fire at the entrance of the tent.

Spurred by thoughts of a possible quick freeze-up, the men put in long, hard hours. In their work, they used a gasoline-powered saw but it was still wearisome, for the trees were as large around as the two of them. The bulk of labor came in rolling the fallen timbers to and down the bank and towing them across to the opposite sand bar. To aid in the crossing they had rigged up a nylon guide line, for the current was swift and the logs liable to catch on snags. A great deal of time was taken up with this, yet there was no helping it. The spruce just happened to be on the side of the river where a raft could not be constructed.

Once on the bar, the logs were then singly rolled back into the water where the men lashed them together with wire and rope. Here was another disagreeable phase of the operation. They wore hip boots but there was no protection for their hands and the raft building had to be done in the bone-chilling water.

Once in a while they needed help to land a log against the current or pole it to the bank and then I would lend a hand, but my main job was to make a comfortable camp. Moss had to be gathered to insulate the rear of the tent where we slept. On top of that went a layer of spruce boughs to cushion and level off the area. Only small, flat limbs were used and laid crosswise so the ends would not protrude.

Such tricks learned from previous camp-outs plus years' accumulation of equipment made the trip more than ordinarily pleasant.

We had long before decided air mattresses to be worth the additional weight and they certainly proved so on this expedition with the men's muscles in need of regenerating each night—and a few of my own, from walking on my knees to do the cooking and the bed making. We had also brought an air pump to blow the mattresses up. This had been acquired against the day metal might be too cold to bring in contact with the lips.

For this year we had added to our gear a custom-made sleeping bag. To get the size we had stretched out side by side on the floor and measured exactly the width of our shoulders and hips and the length from our toes to the top of Fred's head. By these measurements, two pear-shaped, down-filled bags had been made, one to fit inside the other. Exactly enough room for us to turn had been allowed with not a hair's width of extra air space, the prime factor in maintaining warmth. The inner bag was designed with individual bibs fitting snugly around our necks and snap fastened to allow use of our arms. The outer bag was equipped with a zipper all the way around so that we could enclose ourselves entirely in it and yet each regulate openings for breathing. On this expedition we found the outer bag quite adequate. There were both linen and flannel liners which were easier to have laundered than a bag cleaned. As a final note of comfort, we included two small foam rubber pillows.

We had found duffle bags to be indispensable and had filled two large rubberized ones, thereby eliminating miscellaneous boxes and packages. A number of other necessities were the nylon tarpaulin which we spread over the boughs; the nest of metal pans; a lantern instead of candles, and a bucket—all simple things but spelling the difference between hardship and comfort. Further refinements were the rolls of paper towels, scouring pads, pot holders and the clothesline we strung to the ridge pole of the tent for drying socks and dish towels.

We could and did undergo privations if they were necessary but none of us were of the school of thought that they were a requisite of camping.

When there were no restrictions on weight—as there weren't on this trip—I indulged my femininity with nonessential cosmetic aids. There was the plastic bottle of cleanser (which froze and had to be thawed), hand lotion in small tin foil packets and a metal mirror. We had observed that personal appearance becomes increasingly unimportant on a camping trip and I had determined on this one to combat the inevitable de-emphasis. However, it turned out we were all so busy, including Seegoo with his mouse hunting, it was seldom I accomplished more than a face washing, haircombing and a touch of lipstick. Still, just this gave a feeling of being "dressed up" while a shave was a major concession to grooming for Fred. We reached a conclusion that toiletry was relative, just as everything else.

Even with our years of camping under many different conditions there were things to be learned.

That first night I had made a great rick of alder for a fire to welcome the men back from work. But to my disappointment, when lighted, all it produced were clouds of exotically fragrant smoke and a faint sputter. Feeling the returning laborers would place more value on warmth than incense, I spent over an hour trying to bring it to flame— even resorting to the air mattress pump. Then Rod came and with boughs pulled from the base of a spruce, had it roaring in a few moments.

Fred usually shamed Rod and me into getting up by

lighting the "Little Failure" and insisting he had prewarmed the tent. But on our last morning there, the third day of logging, Rod was so anxious to launch the raft that he routed us out at 5 A.M. After breakfast—Rod claimed the eating championship with an even dozen hotcakes—they put the final touches to their masterpiece of rigging and make-do and we started drifting.

The raft was in the lead, the boat tied on the rear. In lone majesty, Seegoo occupied the boat, sitting or lying down with his chin resting on the edge.

We had anticipated trouble in getting down the Siroski and so Rod hand-lined from the shore while Fred and I each manned poles. Without incident, we entered the Una-lakleet River in midmorning. It was overcast and cold with a penetrating off-water cold that cut through long woolen underwear, a double-breasted wool shirt, blanket-lined pants, sweater and alpaca-lined jacket. I soon slipped into my fur parka and, though warm enough, was impressed with the fact that a parka was no garb for sightseeing. A quick turn of the head and one simply gazed at the inside of the parka hood. The habit acquired after a little wearing was to thrust the head forward enough to peer around the edge of the ruff. It gave the effect of the wearer having a stiff neck.

We progressed in large circles, the raft making for the shore at each turn and being nudged away and into another circle. We estimated our average drift to be at three miles per hour and we were elated for we felt we were proving our theory of rafting down and saving gasoline.

Now the landmarks began: Whaleback Mountain; Old Woman Mountain; a tree bobbing in the current; a cairn on a distant hill; fish camps. We welcomed all of these as if they were long-time friends greeting us at the return from a trip.

At noon we pulled on to a beach littered with driftwood. While the men loaded our spruce raft with layers of the "dry wood," I prepared a luncheon on the gasoline stove set up in the boat. We had just begun to eat when a plane flew over—low. It was Wilfred Ryan come to see why we were late getting back. We waved reassurance, he dipped his wings and left us feeling good that we had been missed in the village. Then we were on our way again.

During the long afternoon we were reminded of the days before outboard motors, when the villagers had hand-lined up the river to get to summer camps and drifted down just as we were doing. They, no doubt, hung up on gravel bars just as we did, broadside to the river current.

Now all of us sprang into action, for the pressure of the water was grounding us more securely with every passing ripple. I poled from the raft attempting to rock it while the men with prodigious effort tried to force it upstream. We struggled and sweated and contrived with not the slightest evidence of progress. Our palms began to blister, the men's feet and legs to grow numb from the cold water. We despaired of saving our haul but worse yet of proving our theory. Then, when we were about ready to give up, we noticed a slight easing in resistance. With new determination we forced the entire raft just enough, so that the current caught it and helped instead of hindered us in the setting free. Once more we drifted, but our unplanned beaching had added a couple of hours to the two lost with our noon stop.

It was beginning to get dark when the sound of an outboard motor reached us—far, far away but growing steadily closer. Though the three of us listened intently we couldn't determine the direction. It began to seem as if we were surrounded by motors and then we realized why. Two boats were converging on us, one from the north and one from the south.

This left us in a serious situation. Our raft was without power and we could not put to shore for there were no beaches, only sheer banks on either side. The river was so crooked they would be upon us without warning. Even had there been an open stretch, visibility was poor in the surrounding dusk. There was no time to hunt out our flashlight and we held no hope of the oncoming boats being equipped with spots or starboard and port light.

There was nothing to do but wait: and while we waited, to think of the several near fatal outboard accidents which had occurred on the river; and listen; listen to motors that might sound very near, yet be several turns away or just around the next one.

There was no point in shouting, we couldn't be heard.

Onward they came like roaring monsters out of the night. The first, a racing enthusiast rounding the curve ahead at top speed, his high powered boat bearing directly toward us. And then he saw us. With a swerve, he scooped the water broadside splashing it onto the logs and shot around our end. The raft shuddered and rocked while we squatted for balance and wondered if our lashing would hold. Before we were on an even keel, the second boat, a family returning from camp at a speed to allow their seeing us and putting a margin of water between us, passed.

By then all of us were feeling the effects of the speed-boat scare and, before that, our wrestle to free the raft from the bar. We were ready to stop but the river had turned singularly inhospitable. The bars offered no driftwood, the banks were perpendicular.

Finally, being too tired to go on, we chose a section looming darkly over us and tied to a sapling growing at right angles from its surface. We hunted out the gasoline lamp and pulled ourselves up the bank only to discover our site to be a bed of hillocks. Rather than cast off and look farther, the men planed these off with the only implements available, their axes.

After interminable hacking and fumbling, the tent was up and a fire started at the entrance. And at that precise moment, the wind began to whip around the corner of the tent and to fill it with a dense smoke. We had to decide whether to be warm and suffocate or shiver and breathe, a problem we solved by going to bed straightway after eating.

We awoke to the spatter of rain on the tent. Never had our sleeping bags seemed more seductive. Still, we told ourselves, the theory—the theory had to be proved. With muscles rebelling, we slid out into a raw, damp morning to look upon a stack of soiled dishes from the night before. Our spirits were as the lowering fog. But with breakfast and steaming coffee, enthusiasm began to revive. We decided to pack lunch so we wouldn't have to make any stops and keep going until we "made it."

We were doing well.

We had just sighted the FAA range station some eight hours later when the raft hung up again, this time on a snag. As before, the men improvised and strained to the limit of their strength but all this did not bother them nearly so much as the fact that a boat passed us while we were thus impaled. The passersby had offered help, an offer we proudly refused feeling it would violate the theory. Eventually the raft was pried loose, though with the loss of another hour.

Later, when closer to the village, several others coming upriver for water had offered tows but these, too, we refused.

Instead, we chose to drift without power to the river

mouth while Unalakleet became a gold-edged relief against the lavender sky. We picked out the familiar two-story trading post, school and orphanage. But except for these, the skyline was very much changed from the one we remembered. Two upright oil tanks and a graceful mission spire had been added the past year. The cabins which used to cluster around the square now extended all the way to FAA. Wind chargers sprouting from their roofs and several new clapboard houses gave a-story-and-a-half line to the silhouette. Only the caches on their stilts marked Unalakleet a native village.

We did not pull our raft until starting up the slough.

We had brought down forty-three logs, approximately three cords of wood. If not the largest haul, it was one of the largest of the fall.

The rafting had taken about twice as much time as if we had towed.

By rafting we had saved $6 worth of gasoline.

By being away from the village longer, we had lost two working days and the wages paid to have the dogs cared for during our absence.

Whether or not we proved our theory remained moot.

But of one thing we were certain. The next time, we would do it the native way.

CHAPTER

4

The first thing we did upon arriving back at the cabin was to look at the puppies. So much had they grown we found it difficult to believe they were the ones we had left behind. All of them were walking—a little wobbly, but still locomoting on four legs. The big surprise, however, was a new trick of Geena's. As the more adventuresome of the puppies tumbled out of the house and started off, she would retrieve them by lifting them bodily in her mouth. It made us shudder to see her powerful jaws clamp on a body not much larger than two fists but she never hurt them and the puppies didn't seem frightened by the procedure. Perhaps their thickening coats gave them an added protection.

In the next few days we realized that cutting the logs and rafting them downriver was the smallest part of getting a winter's supply of wood. They now had to be rolled up onto the beach of the slough and sawed into manageable lengths to be transported across the spit. With the combined efforts of Fred and Richard and his garbage cart, this was accomplished. The logs were stacked in full view of our window simply for the pleasure we felt to look upon them. Not only that, the size of our woodpile advanced us in village standing since wealth was measured by such things here.

Once Fred started the sawing into stove wood lengths and splitting, a new job was created—that of stacking split wood behind our stove and keeping an emergency supply in one corner of the outer room. This, we turned over to the lad we had engaged for "dog duty" during our logging expedition. The "dog duty" we now assigned to Howard since he had grown weary of his trash burning assignment. A third boy was hired for trash burning. Thus did we keep harmony in our growing corps of workers and Howard happy and reporting for photography each day. We also liked having the children around and felt it only fair to spread what money there was to be earned among them.

Where we could not directly employ, we did what we could to encourage native initiative. It struck us that Thora might command a better price for her finely sewn skin boots than in the trading posts or from the Native Service. Through a personal contact in a large Midwestern sports shop, we were able to present her with an order for all the boots she could put out. Thora was ecstatic. She envisioned steady employment for a large group of the village women. They would put out such fine work that soon they would be paid double the starting offer. Thora would be able to buy herself a set of teeth and all the sewers would grow rich.

We found Thora's economic theories a bit inconsistent when we tried to pay her for mending some boots for us. I had put a bill in her hand and clamped her fist around it. She just as emphatically laid it on the table, nor could she be persuaded it was her just due. However, when I noticed her eyeing our supply of canned goods and pressed a number of cans into her arms, she accepted them without hesitation. "I don't like money, but grub—that's different," she declared. Then she hurried out to start sewing two sample pairs of boots to be sent to her new customer.

Before the first snow, we received word that Jake was ready to start on the sled and for us to come and take movies. It was one of the most amazing feats of dexterity we had seen.

Jake had a single oak plank twelve inches wide, fourteen feet long and two inches thick laid across a pair of wooden horses. On it were a handful of nuts and bolts and screws, a coiled length of thong and two steel runners. Out of this and this alone, he would fashion a twelve foot sled and there would be some of the board and materials left over.

He began by marking off narrow slats lengthwise of the grain and then sawing them exactly to the line. It was a painstaking task but not nearly as trying for Jake as working in his parka. He could not understand that our film was to depict the way of the "old time" Eskimo and with great reluctance exchanged his modern jacket for a much more photogenic and authentic parka.

Once the ripping was completed there was nothing more to be filmed until Jake should start bending the slats in a steaming process at some later date. He figured to complete the entire job in "half a month's time." Meanwhile, there were the puppies to be recorded, an amusing though exasperating pastime for they were "all over the lot."

In order to keep them from wandering off, we fashioned a corral a single board high. This provided Geena with the chance to get away from them, something she did more often as weaning time approached. We soon came to realize the greatest prerequisites for puppy or any animal photography was patience. We might wait with our cameras for hours only to have them waddle just out of range for the yawn or tussle we might be trying to catch.

Our vigilance was beyond the understanding of most of our native friends. The more sympathetic regarded us with tolerant amusement, others with a measure of disapproval at what they considered a waste of time. But they were also curious. When Dave saw us manipulating large squares of aluminum to catch the fading afternoon sun, he sauntered over.

"Will she bite?" he asked as he approached Geena.

We assured him she would not.

"My, you got fine pups." He picked one up and inspected its paws. "Dark pads. That good. That mean tough feet."

Dave made himself comfortable on a section of log and spent the rest of the afternoon watching us "waste time." When we lifted the top from the puppy house—a measure we had devised to get more lighting on the pups—he could not keep from laughing. "You build puppy house in summer and take off roof in winter!"

Then, being afraid he might have hurt our feelings, he immediately followed up with a pleasantry. Turning to me, he offered his hand, "You got nice teeth, Missis. Look almost good as bought teeth."

Though teeth could not be bought in Unalakleet, most everything else could. There were, in addition to the merchandise of the two trading posts, various home-made items offered at auctions. The first auction of the year took place in mid-October under the auspices of the Eskimo Mother's Club. It was held in the armory—a war surplus quonset used by the National Guard—and the tables brought in for the affair were piled with handsewn baby dresses, home-canned berries, thong, boots, dried salmon, seal oil, hot-pan pads and donations from the two trading posts.

The bidding was brisk and competitive with prices out of all proportion to the actual value of the articles. This show of affluence was probably a continuation of the ancient "potlatch" idea wherein prestige was achieved in the giving of large parties and the bestowing of gifts. Or perhaps it was that no one begrudged the money since the cause was a worthy one—the proceeds going for layettes for the newborn. The $1.80 I spent for a tea towel made out of a sugar sack was small in comparison to some of the bidding. One of the villagers told me proudly she had expended fifteen dollars that evening. There was, however, a difference in the white or "gussok" and the native purchasing. The former paid cash, the latter, a third in cash with the remainder to be made up in commodities for future auctions.

The auction launched Unalakleet's social season. From then on there was a constant round of auctions, benefits, meetings of the Sewing Society, Mission Workers, Alaska Crippled Children's Association, Civilian Defense, National Guards, Home Guards, Village Council, movies at school or at the FAA field, weekly choir practice and PTA meetings. Life was such a social whirl, particularly for the women, that they sometimes broke under the strain. We knew of one instance where a distraught wife had to call her husband off a regular paying job to come home and help organize the household.

Of all the various meetings, the ones with which the natives were most concerned were the Village Council meetings. Here, pressing village problems were dealt with. One action taken had been to make Unalakleet temporarily "off limits" following a clash between village swains and troops from a nearby military installation. The main issue, however, was whether or not Unalakleet should remain in reservation status or vote itself out from under government supervision. We did not attend these meetings, not wishing to become involved in what we felt to be a strictly village affair, but the issue was discussed in every home and it was here we heard the pros and cons.

"We don't own our land on the reservation. We can't sell to anyone who wants to start a business. There'd be more cash in the village if we could sell property," was an often heard declaration.

"But there are no property taxes on the reservation," someone else would point out.

We had asked if there would be enough cash in the village to pay municipal taxes once land was privately owned.

"I don't know. There's more money than there used to be but a lot of people don't think they could pay to go to the hospital or have their teeth fixed. Maybe they couldn't. Maybe there isn't enough cash yet. . . ."

It was a young friend of ours whom we may call Alec, though Alec wasn't his name.

"Why not your own name?" we asked.

"Because everyone laughs at the Eskimos," was the answer. "All the jokes on the radio say Eskimos eat blubber. The magazines say Eskimos live in snow houses."

"You know we wouldn't make fun of the Eskimos," we had answered.

"I know you wouldn't but people would laugh just because we are Eskimos. I don't want my kids laughed at."

We did not pursue the point. Alec had served in the armed forces in a number of different states during World War II and had been asked many silly and a few insulting questions. We could understand why he was sensitive.

Instead of a snow house, which, in fact, no Eskimos in Alaska ever lived in, Alec's home was of board siding. There were several rooms comfortably furnished through mail order houses and on the tables were current newspapers and magazines. The dinner his wife served to us one evening included fried chicken, fresh tomatoes, corn on the cob, peas, potatoes and gravy, homemade bread, pickle chips, olives and apple pie. All of this was made possible because Alec worked for wages. There might be work in nearby military construction or on some Native Service project. There were jobs at the FAA and if not there, large planes came in summer to fly workers out to canneries along the southern coast. When work gave out, there was unemployment compensation. It was then or on weekends, Alec would harness his dogs to go for water and ice and wood just as generations before him had done.

Or Alec might go hunting—geese and ducks and ptarmigan, rabbits in the hills, an occasional moose, a bear in spring emerging from hibernation. Alec had little enthusiasm for the hardships of hunting seal—the tippy kayaks, the cold, or the time one needed to stalk. But as an economic necessity he went in his motor-powered boat out to the floating ice and stalked with a rifle instead of a harpoon. It was when he would return from a hunt, his jacket or sled loaded with fresh meat for his family, that Alec was happiest of all. Still, he would not think of giving up his job for hunting and fishing in the old-time way. His job meant cash and cash bought things he no longer wanted to do without.

There were many "Alecs" in the village, for the Eskimos are a people in transition. The process was sometimes heartbreaking but always fascinating. We were not the only ones to share their agonies and triumphs. Cast in the same role of sympathetic concern were the trader, missionaries, teachers and nurse. It made a strong and enduring bond among us.

Every Saturday found us going to the teacherage for a bath. Usually Floyd Russell, who was principal of the school, would be at his short wave set exchanging directives and information with school personnel in other areas. His teacher wife Lillian, an expert cook, would be baking bread or cookies or pie. After the baths and the baking and the short wave schedule had been met, there was time for sampling the products still warm from the oven along with our coffee—and for visiting.

More often than not our talk turned to art, since Fred was a professional artist and Lillian an enthusiastic amateur. One painting of Lillian's particularly attracted our attention one late afternoon. It was non-representational—a rankly luxuriant splash of colors except for one corner which showed the brown corrugated cardboard beneath. We asked about it.

"Oh that," she said. "That's the leftovers in my tubes. I hate to waste them so I just dabbed them on a piece of cardboard. The corner without any is where they gave out." She told us later she had framed it and given it away to a fellow teacher who thought it quite the nicest thing she had done.

Often the four of us would go next door to the combined home and clinic of the nurse, Iris Jette. Iris had brought not only a delightful Boston accent to Unalakleet, she had also brought a wonderful knowledge of New England cookery. We used to joke about Unalakleet's excess of artists and good cooks because the trader, L. C. Ferguson or "Fergie" as he was called, was quite adept at cooking too.

Iris had traveled widely among native villages. She had seen much and learned from what she saw. Though she was enormously sympathetic to village problems, she was able to meet them with equanimity and good humor. This detachment gave particular insight to her observations.

We did see her usual calm ruffled, however, when we were all over for dinner one evening. She had found only an hour beforehand that her chore boy had been so busy watching a jet plane earlier in the day, he had filled her cookstove with water instead of oil. Though it was late being served, dinner was as always surpassing good. The fowl was a gift from one of the village hunters. It tasted something like turkey, only more juicy. We asked what it was.

Iris shook her head. "I don't know and I'm not asking what or where it came from." There were no further questions from the Russells, the trader or ourselves. We all realized that conservation was a way of thinking that had not yet taken root in the Unalakleet area. Game was still food. And food was to be taken whenever and wherever it occurred since it might not be there for the taking later.

These occasional evenings of companionship in tastefully furnished quarters, carpeted, automatically heated and equipped with hot and cold running water, seemed like extraordinarily pleasant dreams. The reality of this year was in groping our way with a flashlight down the main path to the far end of the village.

It was in the mighty howls of greeting from our sled dogs and the excited yaps of the puppies.

It was inside the tiny, weathered cabin, in the lamp and in the stove waiting to be brought to life and warmth.

These things were the reality of that winter. Yet there was another word for it—peace.

CHAPTER

5

We awoke one morning in mid-October, and we should have known.

The heavy quiet should have told us.

If not that—when the quiet was broken by the joyful shouts of children.

And the plaintive howling of sled dogs.

All these things should have told us as surely as the sight that greeted us when we raised our shades. Snow. Only a light powdering but enough to sugar-frost the cabin roofs and paths.

It was like a powerful electric shock bringing the village to life.

Children did not walk and skip to school, they ran. They threw snow balls or coasted on sleds. They rolled in the snow.

Before the morning was out, the first team had been hitched and raced down the main path. There was no place to go because the slough and river and sea had not ye' frozen over but the driver simply felt an urge with the cc ing of the snow that could not be suppressed.

Our dogs howled after the running team in a frenzy of frustration. All except Seegoo. He did not yet know what it was about. Still, his tail was held higher and he kicked harder after raising a leg than ever before.

By now the puppies had coats of thick down and so the snow did not bother them at all.

They were at a stage of alternating periods of intense activity and deep sleep. At the slightest provocation, or none at all, they would cascade over the ledge of the puppy house chasing and bumping against one another, staging tug wars with each other's tails or playing tag with the wind.

As the puppies waxed fat and healthy, Geena waned. Their sharp little nails lacerated her underside and their teeth raked her teats raw. It was about this time we began to hear an occasional deep-throated growl in the night, followed by piercing yelps of pain which would gradually diminish into small whimpers. Then, one day, we caught Geena in the act of weaning. She was catching a nap in the noonday sun when one little male, who was developing into the most adventuresome of the puppies, nosed to her belly. Geena raised her head and glared balefully in his direction, but the puppy was oblivious to his chill reception and started nursing, whereupon we heard that familiar deep-throated growl and watched in horror as Geena almost engulfed the puppy's head in her mouth. There followed the piercing yelps diminishing into whimpers and—the hasty retreat of the puppy. After witnessing this routine a number of times, we realized she wasn't actually harming them, but was administering a painful crack across the nose with her teeth and, equally effective, scaring them mightily with her ominous growling.

Geena would allow the puppies to nurse occasionally but it was now at her behest instead of theirs. If a puppy had the poor judgment to come back for seconds, or if one happened to scratch her, she would grub the offender out with her nose and send him packing.

We decided Geena needed a rest. We chained her outside the one-board-high corral and took upon ourselves the job of supplementing the puppy diet. We started out with a bottle, nipple and canned milk but during one of these feedings we noticed a pup (it happened to be the adventuresome male again) wobble over to a plate of discarded chicken bones and start gnawing. If the puppies were interested in bones, they were ready for food, we decided.

The next day Howard made fish soup out of trout caught in the Unalakleet River. He did this outdoors using a five-gallon can for a container and one end of a fifty-gallon oil drum for a stove.

"Too bad you not have pups in summer," commiserated Elizabeth who was watching. "Pups learn to eat salmon heads raw in summer, then raw fish not make them sick later. Lot less trouble. Only feed raw fish frozen through."

However, the eagerness with which the puppies lapped up the soup or waded into the pan and then licked it off themselves attested their complete approval of the diet we offered.

This more solid diet did not prevent the adventuresome male and an all white sister from pulling themselves to the top of the board, to teeter there, to flump on their chins, pick themselves up and seek out their mother. She would tolerate their attempts at nursing for only a few minutes and then administer her stern punishment.

We added another board to the corral, not entirely to keep the puppies away from Geena or her away from their food (which she would devour without compunction) but to keep the puppies safe. Wandering around, they might be run over by a sled or hurt by larger dogs and now that our movie was started with seven distinctly marked pups, it was imperative to keep the same cast until the movie was "in the can."

The second board was hardly in place before the adventuresome male was over again. This led to two developments —his being named "Sookgah" (meaning "fast one") and building the fence still another board high.

When Sookgah escaped, he would sometimes call on his father, Seegoo. Seegoo's attitude toward his son could best be described as squeamish, for he would go to all lengths to keep the puppy from coming close but he did not growl or snap as Geena did.

Though our first snow remained hardly long enough for the FAA motor scooter to give all the children a tow on their sleds, it was an added reminder that freeze-up could not be far away. Already slush ice was seen in the river, slush ice which formed an edging like lace along the banks. Since additional snow might blanket the tundra at any time, we decided we should get an entire winter's supply of straw for the dogs. Fred took two of our corps of employees along to help.

I could not go. I had a previous engagement: a birthday party, marking the sixty-fourth birthday of one of our favorite Eskimo friends, Marian Gonongnan. It was she who considered herself to be Fred's foster mother since he had first come to the village over two decades before. She had always been especially kind to him and, later on, to us. The reason he had not been invited to this birthday party was because it was, with one exception, a ladies' affair. The one exception was the postmaster towards whom many jokes were directed about Marian "having work for him next year" and that he would make Marian "rich," since he was in charge of filing social security applications. The postmaster took the teasing good naturedly, ate his refreshments and hurried back to work.

The party was held in a coffee shop operated by Marian's daughter so we all sat around a semi-circular counter while we were served plates heaped with pieces of cake—yellow, white and chocolate plus assorted cookies. There was still a fourth cake, a fruit cake made for Marian by her daughter but it was not cut since it was the favorite of the guest of honor. To her "raisins were candy."

All of the guests were dressed in silk and rayon dresses with cotton hose and dress fur boots. I felt very much out of place in my woolen slacks and plaid shirt, and sorry that I had not correctly anticipated the demands of Unalakleet society.

There was another party within the week, that of Alec's wife. A mother of seven, she was celebrating her twenty-eighth birthday with an intimate little party at night to which she had asked merely four generations of the family and us. In honor of the occasion, Great Grandmother had promised to tell a story. Just as soon as she had eaten her canned fruit and cake, Great Grandmother pushed aside her plate.

"I tell story now because I want to go home."

Though she was wearing modern dress and seated by a porcelain cook stove, there yet remained a feeling of times gone by. Except for Alec, who went into another room, we sat in a circle ringed by shadows from a hanging gasoline lamp. Its hissing was the only sound to break the reverent silence once accorded a great teller of tales. This was her story.

"Once upon a time there were Four Brothers. Four Hunters. And a Sister and a Little Brother.

Every day the Four Hunters go out and hunt caribou. One day they gone.

A man come down from the mountains and see Girl.

'I want to marry with Girl,' he say but Girl not like him.

The Four Hunters come home. The Girl work cutting up caribou and hang it up to dry.

The Brothers go hunt again. This time Girl and Little Brother see flash like sunlight way down coast. It was man in boat. He have copper on his paddle and his headpiece.

'I want marry with Girl,' he said but Little Brother not like Copper Man. Little Brother like Mountain Man.

'No, you not marry with Sister. Other man come first,' Little Brother say so Copper Man went away.

The Four Hunters came back. Next day they not go hunting. Too much work to do on caribou they brought back.

Man from Mountains come down.

'I want to marry with Girl,' he say.

'You like this mans?' Four Brothers asked.

'I not like him,' Girl say.

Just then flashing down coast again. Copper Mans come. Girl saw flashes and run to comb hair (Great Grandmother pretended to comb her hair) ivory comb in those days.

Then Girl comb Little Brother's hair but he muss it up because he like Mountain Man.

Four Hunters say, 'We have potlatch.'

That night, Man from Mountain, Copper Man, Four Hunters all sleep in kashim (the equivalent of a club for Eskimo men) but not Girl and Little Brother.

Copper Man think he do something to get this Girl before he go next day. He make motion with his hands and then (Great Grandmother made a sound exactly like bubbling water) water fill door to kashim. White whale come up and down in water. Next he took mat made of grass over in corner and when he lift it, there was baby seal.

'You want to marry with Copper Man?' Four Hunters asked next day.

'I want this mans,' Girl say. So Four Hunters say all right and they be happy."

This was Great Grandmother's story except for certain clarifications of pronouns since the story teller used "they," "he" and "she" without regard to gender or number. There were no conjunctions or modifiers. Though ages old, it had all the elements—boy meets girl, boy loses girl, boy gets girl. When I asked her daughter, who was the grandmother in the four generations, if this had been a made up story she declared, with conviction.

"Oh, no. Mama not make up story like that."

In the same room was Alec's sister-in-law, born in a tent in February during winter camping, whose grandmother was of the generation born in snowbanks but who would, herself, shortly leave with her GI husband to make her home in the mainland states. Yet, this was not as strange as if she were to return to the village to make her home, for she had been away to a Government boarding school and become used to modern living. If she was not convinced of the truth of her grandmother's story, she was politely attentive.

That night as we walked back to Mik-nik-rok, we were pushed along by a strong wind from the south. When Fred charged outside twice during the night to drive off marauding dogs, it was still blowing. It blew throughout the morning carrying the village sounds of awakening—the splitting of wood, pounding of ice off water barrels and the choruses of the dogs—far out on the tundra.

I was just trimming mold off our slab of bacon for breakfast when there was a tap at the door. It was Harold Charles, a neighbor who was also the "father" in our sled dog movie. He told us there had been an extremely high tide during the night which, abetted by the wind, had flooded the boats along the beach. He had scooped sand and water out of our boat when he had gone to look after his. Fred thanked him with an offer of a trip upriver for water, which was a standard form of payment in the village.

Usually before we could finish breakfast, there would be another caller—Howard. If there was to be photography, we would invite him to join us and discuss the day's shooting and even though he had just left his own table, he never failed to give a good account of himself with our sourdough pancakes. If there was no photographing, he would leave and we would hear him out gathering wood and stacking it in the outer room. Already Howard was growing restive of tending the puppies and since our Number Two boy had tired of the wood chore and quit, we suspected Howard was hinting to exchange puppy duties for the wood detail.

Though Howard didn't know it at the time, his puppy work load was soon to be lightened when we gave two of the females away.

We had come to the opinion that seven was the ideal number to photograph as well as work in a team. This was in agreement with Dave who had told us, "You have nine, eleven, thirteen dogs. You work for the dogs instead of they work for you." Dave had further pointed out that in the days of his forefathers, even though sleds had been clumsy with six-inch-wide runners, only three or four dogs had been used. Dogs then had been so well trained they had responded to arm signals for directions with a single word, "marconah." "Coo" had been the word for "go." With the Gold Rush of ninety-eight, however, came better sleds and mail drivers who started a vogue for dog teams numbering up to twenty.

"Now Eskimo think he have to have lotsa dogs," Dave concluded. But we did not, so. . . .

One pup went to the man who had given Seegoo to us and the other we gave to Rod. We thought the puppies quite a prize—handsomely marked, downy and fat and were, therefore, very much taken aback when Rod reported his puppy had worms. We immediately sent to a veterinarian in Anchorage for medicine but meanwhile word of the situation went through the village and we were offered an interesting variety of local cures.

Andy Bango, the Laplander we had seen on our way upriver to get our winter wood, swore by a mixture of reindeer hair and dog food. He warned us against ever feeding our dogs tomcod—a small fish caught through the ice, declaring them to be a source of worms.

Elizabeth vouched that ptarmigan feathers dipped in seal oil and fed to the dogs had rid her husband's team of worms.

Though we didn't use any of these measures, we were interested to hear of them. In a few days, pills arrived from our Anchorage veterinarian and our puppies were successfully wormed. What medicine was left over became a commodity of trade, since the villagers thought it might have something to do with the unusual size and fine health of the puppies.

One thing the more conscientious of the dog team owners would never do was give their dogs water with any trace of salt in it. We were amazed, then, to see water being gathered from the slough which was close enough to the river mouth to be subject to the tides of the Bering Sea. I asked Elizabeth about it.

"It all right if you get when tide come in and push fresh water from river mouth to slough."

"How do you know whether the water is salty or not," I had wanted to know.

"You rub between fingers," she said. "If it rough, it have salt. If smooth, it all right."

Or, there was also the "soap test."

If soap lathered, the water was salt free. We did not have

any success with either method and finally resorted to boiling a small amount and relying on taste.

By the third week in October, we were breaking ice on the slough for dog water. Though not frozen thick enough to walk on or support dog teams, it was too solid to break through with a boat. The river was still open though getting more shallow and showing wider scallops of ice along the banks each morning. In the face of these forerunners of freeze-up, we felt a large relief when Jake sent word that he was ready to steam the wood for our sled.

For the steaming he had devised an ingenious rig. Using a gasoline camp stove for heat, he boiled water in a five-gallon gasoline can lying on its side and sealed except for a stovepipe outlet. It was into this pipe Jake thrust the slats for steaming. Once they were saturated, they were lifted out and bent over a wooden form and locked in place with a nailed crosspiece, there to take permanent form as they dried out.

"When will you start putting the sled together?" we asked.

"Don't know," Jake told us.

We tried a different tack.

"When do you think it will be finished?"

"Before the snow comes to stay," Jake asserted positively and there we had to leave the matter.

Returning to Mik-nik-rok we met the Russells and Iris Jette, on their way to a wedding anniversary party. All were carrying prettily wrapped gifts and this caused us to wonder aloud how they could meet such occasions so handily when such occasions came so often.

"It's easy," Lillian confessed. "We loaded up with gifts before we came here. All we have to do is pick one out and wrap it. We couldn't begin to buy as expensive presents as the villagers do."

We, too, had been impressed by the amount of money

spent for gifts in the village, such gifts as a cuckoo clock imported from Germany, a chest of silver plate and a hand-tooled leather scrap book which, we were proudly told, "cost forty-five dollars."

Iris theorized that money simply had a different value for the villagers. "They can get parkas and boots and food by hunting and fishing, so what's money for? Luxuries." To Iris' evaluation had to be added the few, very few who had converted entirely to an economy based on cash income. And there might have been exceptions—families still living off the land—but we knew of none in Unalakleet.

Iris met the many gift giving occasions with home baked delicacies, an item which could not very well be evaluated in terms of money. But this we could not do.

With firebrick long missing between the oven and firebox of our Yukon stove, baking was a demanding chore of uncertain results. A pie required rotating the pan a few degrees every five minutes. Cakes and breads were impossible. We contracted with Elizabeth for a regular supply of bread to which she nearly always added "a treat." Elizabeth had decided we should sample the native foods she and her family ate and so she would set aside for us a portion of any she prepared. One of the first "treats" was a jar of preserved blueberries gathered from the tundra in September. Other times, it would be spruce hens the size of ptarmigan and with much the same flavor except for a definite suggestion of spruce which comprise their diet.

We dined well.

Alec had given us geese and ptarmigan and ducks. One duck we were given—not by Alec—we could have done without. The moment it was put into the oven a sickening, oily odor filled the room and we knew we had a "fish duck" —a duck which had subsisted on fish. We had been warned that "fish ducks" could not be made edible, but this we now chose to accept as a challenge. All day we cooked it, changing the stuffing several times and pouring off the excess of oil. The odor became not one whit less nauseating. We could not bring ourselves to taste it hot. We put it out to cool thinking that when cold, the odor and taste might be less disagreeable but they weren't. Cooking the "fish duck" proved to be a complete waste of effort. All we learned was to identify "fish ducks" in the future by their sharp black beaks and shiny black feathers, and to forego the challenge of making them edible.

Besides fowl, there was seal liver which we considered among the world's delicacies and reindeer bought directly from a herder or occasionally from the trading posts.

Salmon trout, fresh caught from the Unalakleet River, was one of our favorite foods and this we had the evening Stephan Ivanoff came to dinner. Having no thermometer to judge the temperature of the fat and no equipment to control it if a thermometer had been used, I learned that frying could be done by ear. The trout, for example, was best prepared at a "medium sizzle" rather than a fast or slow one.

I was especially pleased to serve trout to Stephan because he had taught me how to prepare it when I had first come to Unalakleet to marry Fred. Stephan had been the commissioner and issued us our marriage license, and he had also served as part-time cook for Fred's Uncle, Charles Traeger, when he was running his trading post. It was always fun to visit with Stephan for he had a lively sense of humor, as was shown when he told us about the last family to come down the river before it started freezing over.

"Mischa went upriver for trouts. He have good catch— lotsa trouts, two one-hundred-pound sacks full. But they have hard luck coming down. Mischa, he try to pole the raft the fish were on when pole go up his sleeve and whoops! (Stephan jumped up and demonstrated with a sweeping gesture of his arm) right into the water." By the time he finished the sentence he was laughing so hard tears were spilling from his bird-bright eyes and wetting his large, walrus mustache.

"The water coldest now. Just like ice. Mischa's family stop and make camp and Mischa dry out his clothes. When they start on, Mischa take sack by two corners and pull it and hands slipped or the sack or something and into the water he went again."

Here Stephan doubled up with laughter—soft as was all Eskimo laughter—but none the less merry. Finally, he was able to go on.

"Mischa's family want to laugh but didn't want him to see them so they ducked into brush and laughed and laughed until they was able to come back not laughing."

Maybe it was Stephan's inimitable story telling ability or maybe it was because our fundamental living was affecting our sense of humor but the story struck us as roaringly funny too. Had we been on the spot, I doubt we would have shown the consideration of Mischa's family.

CHAPTER

6

We were having a freak freeze-up.

By October 26, the ice in the slough was thick enough for the villagers to walk on and fish through for tomcod, yet the mouth of the river remained unfrozen. It was "the latest it had ever been open" we were told by older residents. There was no snow at all, that which had fallen having long since disappeared.

We grew restless.

We were anxious to try Seegoo in harness. And though the weather did not follow a normal pattern of development, our puppies did. Faithfully we photographed their growth yet we felt their antics could have been more attractively recorded against a background of snow.

The puppies were entirely weaned and Geena's teats drying up. Now she was starting to teach them to fight. She would lunge at them with a savage snarl, cuff them around and otherwise goad them into fighting back. We thought at times that they would surely cry out but they never did. It sounded fearsome though it was probably regarded by antagonist and antagonized alike as no more than an educational game.

The quickest of the puppies was a small female, all white like Seegoo. Because of her coloring, we named her the Eskimo word for polar bear, Nanook, which was soon shortened to Nanny. Sookgah, the adventuresome male, seemed to have inherited Seegoo's tolerant good nature and refused to take Geena's cuffings seriously. His aggressiveness took forms other than play-fighting, one being his persistent scaling of the fence even though it was by now four boards high. Once "sprung" he would invariably go to see his father, Seegoo—to show his affection in a few friendly nips and to cuddle next to that looming bulk of white fur. The lordly Seegoo, however, could not be bothered but instead of jumping on top of his house to get away, he would turn with a sudden mighty growl which would send the puppy packing from sheer wind velocity if not fear. Seegoo evidently felt his son had reached the age of understanding the spoken word.

Though our photography was set behind schedule by lack of snow, we still found more to be done than time allowed. The snowshoes we had ordered from the Indian village of Kaltag had arrived and to our great amazement and disappointment were strung with string! We did a movie sequence of old-time Eskimo, Accebuck, restringing them with thong although he objected to replacing the string straps.

"My Father say use string so if you go through ice you can break string and get out of them." He told us of going through ice once himself. Of how, as he went down, he snatched off a glove and flung it on the snow so whoever came along would see it and say "Accebuck went down there." The second glove he filled with water and lifted onto the ice reasoning that if a wind came up the glove would

freeze solid and not be blown away. These dramatic measures were taken before he tried, and succeeded, in climbing
out as was attested by his being there to pose for us.

A smaller sled we had contracted for was brought over
completed and this had to be treated with linseed oil. At
the same time we equipped it with a "hold"—an iron pipe
lashed vertically to one of the rear uprights through which a
crowbar could be thrust into the ground. In this manner the
sled could be anchored whenever the driver wished to leave
it.

While we were occupied with these preparations for winter, the village was bustling with preparations for one of the
biggest events of the season—a wedding.

The groom's mother, Martha Nanouk, came over to invite
us for that night at seven. Actually, the affair had been
scheduled for two weeks but had been postponed because
the wedding dress had failed to arrive from a mail-order
house. We had known of it even before that since Theresa,
the bride-to-be, worked for Lillian and had given notice,
though not several day's notice. Theresa had, in fact,
planned to work up to the time of the wedding, even
preparing the Russell's evening meal but when the date was
finally set, Lillian insisted she take at least the afternoon
off. Once prevailed upon, Theresa went directly to help her
future mother-in-law scrub down the kitchen where the wedding reception would be and where the young couple would
stay until they moved into a house of their own.

There was no pampering of the bride and there was no
prenuptial chatter between Theresa and Lillian though they
maintained a very friendly relationship. "It's as if the bride
was someone else," Lillian told us and gave up showing any
interest since the indifferent attitude she met with made her
feel as if she were prying. We had met the same lack of
response once when I had asked an expectant mother the

date her baby was due and the question had been completely ignored. I learned later that there were those who not only refused to discuss it but would make no layette in advance for fear the child would be stillborn and the baby clothes would be "burial clothes." Perhaps there was some such fear in talking of a marriage too, but we never learned of it if there was.

The ceremony was held at the mission orphanage which was this year being used as a high school. In one of the classrooms appropriately decorated with white paper bells and handmade roses, the best man and a nervous groom took their places before Missionary Maynard Londborg. Then, to the strains of the wedding march coaxed out of an embattled upright piano by the missionary's wife, Lorraine, the bride's attendant entered followed by the bride on the arm of her father.

As becomes a bride she was trembling so much her bouquet of crepe paper flowers shook visibly. There was the troth, a prayer, a hymn and they were pronounced man and wife and the kiss with which the groom saluted his bride was no less ardent than that of any young lover.

The couple hurried to the rear of the church to receive congratulations from the guests whose departure was somewhat delayed, while Martha delivered an earnest exhortation in native dialect to bride and groom to lead a good life and shun liquor and evil ways. We didn't know what she said until later, but the couple were moved to tears then, and again when the bride's mother spoke to them at length, also in native dialect.

Next came the reception at Martha's home. It was held in two rooms no more than ten by twelve feet and the handling of the guests in the space available was a near miracle of efficiency.

Guests had been invited by tens with the "gussoks" (non

native) comprising the first shifts. Incomers were seated in the bedroom and when plates were served with portions of jello, ice cream, cake, cookies and Halloween candy names were called off one at a time. We felt complimented because we were included, not in the first shift which was all "gussok" but in the second shift which was "gussok" plus Alec and his wife.

As soon as we had eaten, we left to make room for the next guests which in all numbered eighty-five.

The wedding was no sooner over than came Halloween when villagers went all night calling for tricks or treats. We were ready to receive, having ordered candy for the children by air from Anchorage and made punch and cookies for the older Halloweeners. Though every house was called upon there didn't seem to be any thought of tricks, only treats.

The children showed active imagination in their costumes which were odd and colorful combinations of various articles of clothing. Some wore a blue glove on one hand and a green one on the other or an unmatched pair of socks. Boys wore their mother's bright scarves around their waists or their sister's reddest dress—often on hindside-before. Girls wallowed in big brother's trousers and big brothers squeezed into small sweaters. One and all, however, ensconced their heads in brown paper sacks decorated with grotesque faces sketched in crayon and charcoal.

When we heard them knock (very softly for the goblins they were supposed to be) we would call to them to come in and then we would exclaim in great length over their getups until they would turn against the wall to hide their embarrassment and pride. None of them would utter a sound or otherwise give away their identity until we gave up guessing. Once that happened, the paper bags would be lifted off and identities announced amid gales of giggles. And then everyone would help themselves to candy, being careful not to take more than one piece until urged to have more, and thank yous were said so properly as to make these far Northern goblins a model for Halloween goblins everywhere.

One big goblin with his head concealed in a large sugar sack came in carrying a guitar. He gave us no time to admire or guess. He walked straight to our bench and breathing heavily, but not saying a word, seated himself and started singing in Native. There were two songs, one an Eskimo love song sung in a crooning minor key at once poignant and melodic. When the last note was sung we were silent. This wasn't meant to be a Halloween prank and we didn't quite know how to respond. Off came the mask and to our utter astonishment, we recognized a neighbor whom we had spoken to for years, yet this was his first call on us. We helped him to juice and cookies and he reminisced of another Halloween when he had disguised himself and gone to the home of his wife's parents. So good was his disguise they had no idea who he was and his father-in-law even took him for someone else. When they found out who he was they were so ruffled, they went into the other room and stayed there, even while he had his coffee.

Once during the evening we spiked the spooks.

Having heard a suspiciously familiar giggle in the outer room, Fred snatched an Eskimo dance mask from the wall and handed it to me. Hastily I put it on and stood so that the door hid me as the goblins trooped in. Then, as they stood silently waiting for Fred to guess who they were, I jumped out with what I hoped was a blood chilling "boo." Our goblins were so startled, a few screamed while the others broke into nervous chattering and laughter. Howard, for whom the surprise had been staged, recovered quickly.

"Boy! I feel cold hands on my back when you yell," he said. And another had felt "needles in her lip." Both described their fear in terms of physical reaction as we had heard other villagers do—grown-ups as well as children.

Halloween was the first time we had seen Howard for several days. With fine fall weather still continuing, the urge to be off playing was stronger than the urge to report to us. When he would come after such an absence, we never asked questions or reproached him, for that would make him unhappy and we didn't want to work with an unhappy model. Since Howard had become bored with tending the puppies we had let him take over the wood detail. Number three boy switched from burning trash to care of the dogs which involved feeding the puppies dried meal three times daily and the big dogs once in the evening.

Of all our retainers, Elizabeth was the most faithful. She provided us with our weekly supply of baked goods and she did our washing and never once did she miss. Sometimes she would come early in the morning with loaves of bread still warm from the oven. Then Fred would leave off splitting wood or bringing the dog pans in to melt the frozen water or whatever chore he happened to be doing and join us. We would cut off thick slices, smear them with butter and with no difficulty put away half a loaf along with several mugs of freshly made coffee.

Many visits, if in the morning or late afternoon, were now in the cozy glow of lamplight. For some time we had been preparing and eating our breakfast by lamplight as the sun didn't begin to rise until after eight and by four-thirty in the afternoon was gone again.

Often Elizabeth would bring her four-year-old adopted son, Jonathan. There was another child, a daughter of junior high school age, a "real child" as blood children were often called. And there were three others—a boy of around ten and two preschool girls for whose care Elizabeth received a monthly check from the welfare department.

Elizabeth idolized her Jonathan and when he would oc-
cupy himself with articles on our shelves she would declare proudly, "He got busy hands." We never saw him rep-
rimanded with more than the softest "no, no," nor for that
matter did we see any of the village children punished with
the exception of Alec's. Still, Martha assured us, "Eskimos
do punish their children." Just not in front of people.

If Jonathan became especially restless and noisy, Elizabeth might say, "Jonny, I let you go outside now." "Let"
she used more in the sense of suggesting—sometimes bordering on a command—yet it had the sound of gracious
permission. Elizabeth was void of temper or vindicative-
ness. When a villager of some standing had once derided
her on some mistake in written English, she had rushed
home and "let" one of the children take him a gallon of
blueberries. "He never treat me mean after that," she told us
happily. Besides giving us a familiarity with native foods,
she saw to it that we benefitted from the knowledge she
had inherited and acquired living in the far North.

She it was who pointed out I should not wear "water
boots" at this time of year. Water boots were of seal skin
which had been especially treated and scraped free of hair,
and were processed to repel water. With little likelihood of
"soft weather" for sometime, she suggested the boots be set
aside until really needed, since the brittle skin might chip
with constant use. These things I had known but had put
off doing anything about. Now, in deference to Elizabeth's
concern, we sent for one of our favorite sewers of boots,
Thora.

Thora came bustling over in great good spirits grinning
widely with toothless gums. She measured my feet by the
length between her thumb and outstretched forefinger, and
while doing it made many a joke about their great size. The
Eskimos being a small people had small feet and Thora

could not reconcile the fact that our feet were more in proportion to our size than Eskimo feet would have been. But we were good friends and she knew she could tease us about our outsized extremities and we knew we could tease her about being proud of her small feet, which she indeed was.

We also ordered a pair of "muh-mee-luks" for Fred. These were another type of waterproof boot—warmer than mine and sturdier. With them the hair of seal was left on, turned inside from foot to knee and outside from knee to hip. The skins had usually been soaked in seal oil to give them added water proofing.

While she measured, we asked Thora how she was coming along on the sample boots for the sporting goods store in the States. Her mouth dropped open. She drew in her breath and slapped her hand to her cheek in dismay.

"I forget all about it," she confessed. "Is it too late?"

We told her we didn't think so.

"I make them soon as I finish these for you."

"Kop-see-nik?" (How much?) I asked.

She sandwiched my hand between her own and placed it against her cheek. "Do not ask me about price," she said. Then, suddenly self-conscious about her show of emotion, she dropped my hand and laughed. "You might not buy them!" With this sally she left but we were not worried. We knew Thora would be fair.

It was about this time—before winter spread its shining sheath—that the big plane came to take the village youths who were members of the National Guard for a two week's encampment. Extra drills had been ordered for many days to get the men in shape. And these were taken with grave seriousness, for who among them had not looked east at the endless tundra and west over a surging gray sea or a vast expanse of ice and not felt his isolation. Not only did the

Seegoo and all the pups spend the night with us.

Our home for the winter: dinner time.

Our litter of Malemute puppies nursing.

The Soxie sisters sculpturing "Mr. Machetanz."

Walking ahead of the dogs to break trail.

Harold thought the chain saw a great invention.

After steaming the wooden slats for the sled, they are placed over a form to dry.

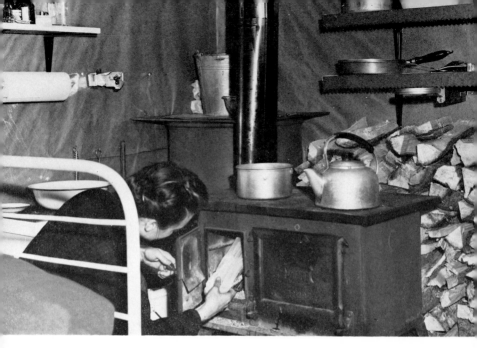

Our Yukon stove; water drum; and our lavatory—washstand with catch bucket beside it.

Rafting our winter wood supply from up the Siroski River.

Our home and "Dogtown".

Frozen eyelashes.

National Guard furnish tangible protection with the rifles issued its members, but uniforms provided clothing and "Guard" pay was another source of cash for the village.

As training had accelerated, so had interest throughout the village. Children devised a new game called "National Guard" which they played with wooden guns and when the time of departure finally came, the troupe was followed out to the airstrip by a throng of relatives, wives and sweethearts. Among the followers were Elizabeth's husband and his daughter, Blanche. We met them going out as we arrived at their door for Blanche's twelfth birthday dinner.

Elizabeth used the same method of "shifts" as Martha had at the wedding reception. The guests (Elizabeth's friends and a close school chum of Blanche) were seated in the bedroom and called by turn to the table. There was a delicious moose and noodle casserole and extremely generous portions of ice cream and cake. We were nicely served on pretty plates in an impeccably clean kitchen. Elizabeth was just as hospitable when I dropped by a day or so later and her family was lunching on a dried salmon from which they would pick bites to dip in seal oil.

"Just in time," she joked, for she knew I had not yet developed a taste for seal oil. Elizabeth knew fish and seal oil were good for her family, it was economical and besides all that, some native foods were too good to be cast aside.

As soon as lunch was over, the children went out to play and Elizabeth set to making thread. She made it out of sinew off the back of a reindeer. To separate the strands she used her teeth—the most important tool in the making of sinew thread she told me. By rolling two of these strands on the back of her hand and at the same time twisting them together, she had much stronger thread than she could buy. While we sat at a table and chatted, her husband, Gene, was putting a new canvas cover on his kayak in the other room. "Woman's work," he complained, but all the women in the village who had strong enough hands to do it and knew how were busy.

Once the canvas was stretched tight over the frame, he would coat it with a waterproof paint. He was anxious to get the job done so he could go hunting for the prized spotted seal which were in the area only at this time of year. That he had been successful in hunting the more common hair seal was attested by a seal skin hanging from the ceiling which, having been cleaned and scraped and filled with air, looked like an oversized balloon. It was called a "poke" and one day Elizabeth would make it into a knapsack for Gene, she told me.

I asked her about the relative merits of furs for "inside" parkas which were, as their name suggested, worn inside an outer parka. She suggested duck or bird feathers quilted. Rabbit skin was nice but would shed. Ground squirrel was the nicest of all, though more expensive. Elizabeth had trapped for squirrel the spring before. That was the best time because the fur was best even though it had "bugs." She had put her traps in front of a hole weighted down with stones so the eagles wouldn't carry them away and then she had covered them with moss for camouflage. But, "the fun was over when it came to skinning."

For an "inside" parka, there was also fox. It was warm and bulky. Martha had one out of fox.

"That too hot for me," Gene broke in. "That only for womans."

While we were thus pleasantly passing the time, daughter Blanche burst in.

"Ma! Ma! The tomcod are thick. Where is the tomcod pole?"

Both Elizabeth and Gene hurried to look. Gene found it,

a two foot long pole with a long line tangled and full of knots.

"Womans did it," he commented as he handed it over to Blanche. "Woman's job to fish for tomcod."

Elizabeth put aside her sinew to hunt another pole and together we went to the slough. I hesitated at the edge of the ice. It was so clear one could read the print on the tin cans lying on the bottom of the slough. In fact, the ice was so transparent, there didn't seem to be any at all. But the number of fishing women and children was assurance the ice was strong.

The run was getting thicker. Those who had been kneeling on their knees or sitting on sacks, jumped up in excitement and started pulling tomcod in as fast as they could take up the slack with the help of a stick held in their free hand. Word spread and men and boys, Gene among them, came running with shovels, rakes, boxes—anything to scoop out the fish. When the run was over, the glistening pyramids of fish were loaded into wheel barrows and hauled home. Most of them would be strung on loops of grass to hang like leis on the fish racks to dry.

Elizabeth picked up a nice plump one half a foot long.

"They're best just now," she said. "This full of liver and eggs maybe." Laying it on a board she slit it open with her ooloo, a half-circular knife. It was indeed full of roe. "Liver extra large this time of year, yellow too," she showed me. "I fix some for you."

The bowl she sent home with me that evening proved to be one of the outstanding delicacies of the year, even though we had been told, "Eskimos like tomcod soup only with seal oil and only if raised poor." We thought the roe as good as that of shad and the livers tasted more like smoked oysters than liver.

It had been such a large run that the villagers spoke of it for several days. One of them who had been going north along the coast for water at a still open creek had run into the tomcod so thick they had sheared the pins on his outboard motor.

The sea was now frozen for a distance of an eighth of a mile, but the beaches were lined with tomcod the gulls had picked up and dropped. When Dave came by to look over the pups, he told of a neighbor woman who took her pole and bucket "to have some fun hooking" and found the fish so thick there wasn't any room for her hook!

He stood by the pen to which we had added a fifth board.

"Pups can climb this high now?"

"Yes. We just added the last board but Sooky (Sookgah) still gets over."

"He want to get out and go. He may be leader." Dave advised us to cut down from three to two meals a day since the pups would have to go through a process of stretching their stomachs before they could eat enough to go on one meal like the big dogs.

The talk turned to Seegoo. We told Dave we hoped to make him leader of our working team.

"How old is he?" Dave wanted to know.

"Five years."

"That's old to start training." He inspected a paw while Seegoo, hoping for a good petting, rolled over on his back. "Good big paws. Hair between the pads. That good."

"We heard dogs with humps on their noses make good pullers, so maybe Seegoo will be a good leader?"

Dave shook his head. "Most important things is whether he want to lead or not."

We asked about training.

"You might go out with him alone first. Maybe have to wait for snow. Most dogs scared of clear ice."

"Do you suppose the snow will ever come?" I asked. We were beginning to fear this would be the year Unalakleet wouldn't have a winter. But we needn't have worried.

In mid-November we began having "Man Winter" though
there was still no snow. One Native oldster who had waited
for freeze-up to return from his summer fish camp, reported
driving his dogs every turn of the river, since there was no
snow on the portages. This was the first time he could remember doing that and he was in his eighties. With the
temperature ranging from zero to ten above, certain changes
in our living had to be made.

First, there was the problem of a room so cold in the morning there would be a skim of ice to break on the canned
peaches and fruit juice. Eggs on our lower shelves froze
solid and cracked overnight. Fresh produce was always soggy
from being frozen and thawed and potatoes which we had
kept on the floor turned black. We found that the three feet
between the floor and the table top usually was the difference between freezing or not, so moving all the perishables
onto the table at night became a regular ritual.

Fred evolved another ritual. After pulling out of our flannel cocoon (we were using our sleeping bag liner) into the
bitter cold of early morning a couple of times, he began

emptying the Yukon stove of its embers every night and laying a fire before we went to bed. In the morning, all that was necessary was to reach out from the bed and light the stove from where he lay.

My signal to get up and about came when the coffee which I had measured and set on the stove the night before began to perk. I found I could postpone the ordeal by some fifteen minutes if I filled the pot with ice, though I felt guilty about doing it until I found out Fred was getting up by the clock which during the night would slow down with the cold and sometimes stop entirely.

By 6:30 every morning the fire was lit, the battery radio turned on and the strains of the "Star Spangled Banner" coming through over the Armed Forces Radio Service Station in Nome. This was followed by setting up exercises "Up! Down! Up! Down!—Now the other eyelid."

During the colder weather, reception became more acute with the result we would stay up later and later, listening to stations as far off as California and once even Texas. The clearest station on our radio at all times was Radio Moscow putting forth propaganda twenty-four hours a day. It gave us an added consciousness of our closeness to Russia and if for any reason the Nome station went off the air, we kept our radio tuned to the station until it came on again.

When the coffee perked and I arose to cook breakfast and put up the shade, it would be to a window coated with frost so thick we could not see out. Still with the glow of the lamp and shadows flickering on the ceiling from the stove draft, there was a good cozy feeling to it all. Quarter-inch frost gave a head of paste to the nails in our "porch" which became a perfect deep freeze.

Our sewage system changed from chemical to lining the toilet with moisture-proof dog feed sacks. Solidly frozen, these were easily disposed of. One crowning aid to comfort was our removable toilet seat which made a prewarming behind the stove possible.

One night there did come a powdering of snow which was, however, gone by morning. We happened to see it because we were up during the night chasing off marauding sled dogs. During the winter we suffered much more from lack of sleep due to stray dogs than from the cold.

With the river now frozen hard enough to go on, we decided to harness Seegoo to our smaller sled and go upriver for ice.

Seegoo was delighted that we were singling him out. While we put his harness on, he rolled over to have his chest scratched and thumped his tail madly. When we pulled him up and told him to "gih" (go), he looked around in his friendliest fashion and trotted back to us at the rear of the sled. Fred led him forward and we again gave the command to "gih." Again the same thing. And again. He simply could not comprehend the idea of going forward and away from us, his entire training having been the opposite—to sit, to stay, come, or lie down.

Finally we gave up and Fred trotted beside him down to the banks of the slough. There, Seegoo balked at the transparent ice. He would stand at the edge, look into the depths, put forth a paw to make certain there was ice and then back off. Fred coaxed and walked ahead. It was no use. Then I jumped out and joined Fred. Seegoo barked in a frenzy. When we started to walk away from him he couldn't stand it. He would have let one of us go, but not both. He inched onto the ice, slipping, sliding, but yet advancing. As soon as we were onto the river ice, I again came to the back of the sled and Seegoo skidded along beside Fred.

We had chosen a bad day for his "shakedown cruise." Not only was it two above, but there was a wind blowing. Fred was literally blown off his feet several times and Seegoo and the sled and I skidded diagonally across the ice. Still, bitter as it was, I was surprised when Fred told me my face was getting frost-bitten, a condition quickly alleviated by warming with the bare hand.

We went up past the FAA range station, since the ice there wouldn't be affected by the tide or contamination from the village. One of the villagers was already busy sawing and lifting out with tongs large blocks of ten inch thick ice for school. He had quite an impressive pyramid of lovely, clear ice, more than he could possibly haul away in one load, yet he would leave it to be gathered at a later date with no fear that anyone would help themselves and no one would. Though the school, teacherage and clinic were all equipped with running water, it was brackish and so they procured their drinking water from ice just as everyone else did.

Others came, one couple pushing their sled. They had given up fishing in summer, and with no fish for dog food had had to dispose of their team. Another sled was pushed up—slats broken and in need of lashing. Both young men were wearing government-issue felt "Bunny" boots. They no longer hunted for seal, and even if they had, their wives would not have known how, or cared to make the skins into boots. Some teams passed us going farther upriver for ice and wood, and one villager was on his way to trap mink for "a couple of weeks or as long as the dog food holds out."

On the way back to the village we sped swiftly along with the wind to our backs. Both of us rode in the sled and Seegoo galloped ahead, keeping the towline taut as a veteran. I thought he was learning to run in harness, but Fred surmised he was merely keeping the sled bumper off his haunches. He did so well we refused an offer of a lift by a FAA mechanic who was out with a snow tractor and sled.

Back at Mik-nik-rok, Sarah had a fire going and was busy with the dishes and visiting with a friend, Ruthie. We hurried in, after unharnessing Seegoo, for our boots were wet from the chopping and sawing ice and there had been no snow to dry them off with.

The moment Fred entered the door, both Sarah and Ruthie looked at him as if they were about to burst with a happy secret. Cutting their eyes at him, they chorused, "No snow."

They were teasing him for being wrong in predicting snow the day before. It had been part of a game while they were doing dishes. Fred had several times stretched out on the cot and put on an act as a medicine man. Mumbling in an unknown tongue (even to him) pressing his eyeballs with his fists and using me as a cohort, he would correctly call out some object they had decided he must guess. Of course, all of this was by prearrangement between Fred and myself, as they no doubt knew, but they were piqued at not being able to guess our formula and that Fred passed it off as "magic." It, therefore, gave them especial delight to point out that he had lost his "magic," at least in predicting weather. They liked the game so much we would play it two or three times, then Fred would pretend to be exhausted from his efforts and leave them begging for "just one more time."

Before we could play this day, however, we had to take our boots off and stuff them with grass so they would dry out more quickly. Tomorrow the soles would be stiff and shrunken and have to be softened by kneading around an old axe handle we saved for just that purpose. We had heard Elizabeth say "feet don't get cold in soft boots like in hard" and we knew this to be true.

"You go through ice?" Sarah wanted to know.

"No," Fred told her. Then, "Did your father ever tell you about the time he went through ice?"

"Papa go through ice?" Sarah asked incredulously.

"He surely did. Didn't he ever tell you?"

Sarah shook her head. "He never tell me."

"Well, he told me about it. He told me he would try to climb out and the ice would keep breaking. He broke it with his elbows to try and get a solid path to climb out, until he tore his parka sleeves and gloves off and his arms were bloody. He climbed out, but his arms have been crippled since."

Sarah listened round-eyed. When she listened, she listened so completely she stopped everything else. "Papa never tell me," she marveled softly.

We had known of other successes unrecounted, of a high school girl receiving a coveted honor, yet her family only learning of it indirectly. Any telling of personal achievement might seem like bragging and that was unacceptable socially. The few that did it were invariably laughed at—the worst form of social censure.

Sarah had "news" for us that day. Her sister had given birth to a baby boy. It was premature and it might not live, but it was quite an event for there was only one male—a brother in a family of several sisters and sisters' children.

The next day we took Seegoo out again. And the next—using a guide line on his collar so he would learn to "Gee" and "Haw."

Howard watched us leave on these runs and asked to go along to drive the team and help get water and ice, instead of bringing in split wood. Since we were anxious to have Howard learn to handle dogs, we were very happy to make the change. Number three boy took over Howard's wood chores and we hired a new boy, Number four, to feed and clean up after the dogs.

Taking note of the rapid rate at which requests for changes of duty came in, Fred added the motivation of a shotgun at the end of the year, should Howard stay with us the entire time. A part of the cost would be paid out of his regular wages, and a part of the cost we would assume as a bonus.

Howard was all for the idea. Tangibles such as food and a gun seemed to mean much more to him than what money might buy.

Fred and Howard had just gone off with Seegoo when I saw Elizabeth taking her frozen wash from the line and leaning it like boards against her house. This was my signal to take mending and go over for a visit while she ironed. Only today she wasn't ironing. The clothes had to dry out more after they thawed and so she chose to make a mat from grass instead.

First she had gathered a special kind of grass. It was a flat grass—not hollow like that used for dog houses and boots. This mat grass had a sharp point in the base which was about four inches long and which would make the new shoot next year.

Kneeling on the floor, Elizabeth divided the grass into bunches the size each segment of the mat would be. Then she made wisps of a half dozen strands and started weaving over and under the bunches. It made a very attractive mat. I decided to make one too and went straightway to the place Elizabeth directed to gather grass to start on one that same afternoon.

Elizabeth was glad for company. She was "feeling heavy." A girl she had once looked after for the welfare department and who was now grown had returned to the village and come straight to her. Though Elizabeth's two-room home was filled with five other children, she hadn't the heart to turn her former charge away. While she was telling me about it, her "welfare" son came in and went out again to split some wood.

"He never made trouble. He always made me feel warm inside."

I told her about the new baby, the premature which had not lived through the day.

"They say sometimes baby lost because mother exercise too much," Elizabeth commented. There was a pause. "I know one woman not believe that. She have two babies, no fathers. She exercise all the time. Not lose a one." Our eyes met and we laughed. We had such a fine understanding.

I was having trouble with my mat. Somehow it was getting larger at one end or smaller at the other. Elizabeth gave it a deft pull here and there, loosened some strands, tightened others and had it straightened out in a few moments. Then she went on.

"That girl make fun of me one day on the path. Married two years and no children. What kind of marriage is that! I tell her she have two children and no marriage."

"What did she say then?"

"She say, I'm still young. I bear children. She say right!"

There was a clamor of sled dogs. It was Gene returning from getting a load of wood. He had been upriver after "green" wood (growing spruce).

"No dry wood (driftwood) big enough to bother with this year. Just squaw wood," he reported. Still, he had already made three stacks down on the beach, to be transported by sled when there was snow. "Al-ah-pah (cold)." He took off his glasses which had steamed up and walked over to the stove. Gene had been in a boating accident and sent away to a hospital where a steel plate had been put in his leg. This, he said, bothered him, especially in the cold. It had left his leg stiff, yet he would drive the dogs and hunt as most of the men.

The cold continued unbroken. The dog water pans were solidly frozen each morning and for the first time we noted ice on the dogs' whiskers. I happened to mention it several days later when Thora came by with our completed boots.

"Ha!" she exclaimed. "I tell you real story of ice on whiskers." She settled in her favorite spot on the floor with her back against our sea chest. "Three men stranded on ice. They get thirsty. Nobody come. They get thirstier and thirstier. One of them have mustache and he would suck the ice on it from his breath. Finally one mans could not stand it any longer. 'I give you wolverine skin for ice off your mustache.' The mans with mustache say 'one half mustache.' The other mans say 'all right.' So mans with mustache work real hard making moisture and"—here Thora used a magnificent gesture—"raked the ice off half his mustache and give to him."

Then Thora unwrapped the mukluks she had made for me. They were lovely, with light young oogruk (giant seal) soles, reindeer tops trimmed around the rim with beaver and red felt. They were tied with balls of red and white yarn. They would be my dress boots. Fred's muh-mee-luks proved to be too small. Thora simply couldn't believe her measurements were correct and not wishing to offend him had altered them. Now she would have to do the soles over. Still, she knew us well enough to joke about it. She showed me the correct way to lace my new mukluks— behind the heel, then around in front of the ankle.

I did not realize there was any special significance to the tying until Dave was over Thanksgiving and noting my boots exclaimed, "You tie boots like woman in old days. Good." He went on to explain that men tied their boots differently from the women—with the ties sewed to the forward portion of the boot and crossed over the instep, laced through loops below the heels and then around the ankles.

Before Dave left, we went out to look over the pups.

He exclaimed over how nice and fat they were. He asked us again how old they were and when we told him ten weeks he expressed surprise at their size. "You should start taking them for walks on the tundra."

"But we thought there was a village ordinance against stray dogs."

"There is," Dave admitted. "Still you got to make good strong dogs. You take them out on tundra."

He suggested a two mile walk but that we should keep them off the ice as they might fall and become afraid or even break a leg. The ice was at a very bad stage. There had been another high tide the night before which, abetted by a southwest wind, had caused extremely high water. The sea ice had been literally lifted up and dashed against the shore, leaving debris and one hundred-pound chunks littering the coast. It would make difficult sledding later on. The high waters had crumpled the ice at the river mouth giving the appearance of break-up, and it had made an island of the slough ice by breaking it loose from the banks.

The flats across from the slough were inundated and the smell of fresh salt water was strong in the air.

Richard had worked long past midnight pulling boats higher up on the banks of the slough with the school tractor. Even so, one boat had been completely buried and another ruined as it was smashed against the barges up on their way for the winter.

We all wondered if the tide had reached to the ice laboriously cut and stacked upriver. Now that the mouth was open, there would be no going upriver until it froze again. With a certain shortage of water to be faced, an announcement was made in church that anyone in need might use the well of the local bush pilot.

For us, the worst aspect was the holding up of our movie making. Seegoo must be trained and pictures taken of the big team on trail. Yet there was no snow for dog teaming or even ice to run Seegoo.

In the middle of this doleful turn of events, there was one bright spot. Jake came with our large sled. And hadn't Jake said he would have it completed before the snow came to stay.

CHAPTER

8

It didn't snow the next day, nor the next, nor the day after that. Each morning we would raise the shade to scrape a peep hole in the frost and peer hopefully into the darkness and—there would be no snow.

One morning, I noticed a movement in the bin where extra straw for the doghouses was stored. When Fred hurried out to investigate, there was Sookgah bouncing around with the blissful absorption of a trampoline artist. After that we could not keep him in the pen even though Fred nailed an overhang all around the top board of the fence. He would simply leap high enough to lock his forelegs on the overhang and then pull himself up like a monkey. All the while he would be giving forth cries pitiful to hear as the rest of the puppies would gnaw on his hind legs and tug at his tail. If his brother and sisters couldn't escape, it appeared they did not want him to either. They would give the precocious Sookgah the same hostile treatment when he would descend into the pen after spotting Fred coming with the food sack. The entire litter would set upon him and with fearsome ferocity roll him over and give an impression of tearing him to bits. Although the attackers sounded bloodthirsty as a banzai charge, no injury ever resulted or at least none we could detect. Once the food pan was set down, they would all completely forget the mayhem and romp to the common trough to eat side by side in peace.

Sookgah displayed Seegoo's general good nature and capacity for affection. As soon as he was out of the pen he would head straight for our cabin and if we happened to open the door, would dart in before we could block his way. Or, if it happened we were outside working, he would rush eagerly over for a pat. We noticed that he was sensitive to noises and asked Dave about it.

"If I were picking a leader, I would pick one who jumped at noises," Dave said. "They learn the sound of 'Gee' and 'Haw' quicker."

Since Seegoo shared the same sensitivity to sound, we hoped what Dave said would prove to be correct but there was no way of finding out until the ice was solid again or the snow came.

Finally it did come—the next to the last night of November and when it did, it was as if all the storms we had missed had somehow been combined into one.

It came as a great, greedy white monster with a roar and a howl and a breath of searing cold. It pounced upon us and clamping our tiny cabin with long, icy fangs shook it until the windows chattered in fear and the chimney sounded possessed of a sub-arctic poltergeist. Outside, the swirling black maelstrom continued the night long. Inside, swathed in our sleeping bag, we listened with smug satisfaction to the fury that could not touch us. We listened and we knew from the sound and from the feel of the storm what to expect next morning even though it was too dark to see out when we awakened and started our day. We knew when we entered the porch and saw there miniature snow drifts tracing the pattern of each crack in the outer door. And when we opened that door to find Sookgah plastered with ice like a coat of mail waiting to come in. Seegoo was sitting forlornly outside his house, it having been completely filled with snow.

That day we shoveled—with our ruffs turned in so the gusts of stinging snow would not permeate the fur. We shoveled out the puppy house and all the dog houses, and then Fred nailed curtains of gunny sacks over the entrances. We shoveled clear our own door and the west window where the snow was a solid eight feet up against the cabin. We shoveled out a pile of split spruce and took it inside and placed it on the stove to thaw and dry. The heavenly incense it gave off was an odor we would forever associate with that winter and living at Mik-nik-rok.

Contrary to their eagerness to "go" at our first show of snow back in October, the dogs were curled up, noses in tail until their houses were cleared and then they disappeared into them completely. They evidently did not find the cutting wind any more comfortable than we did.

That night we were bone-tired but it was a good tiredness —the kind that comes when one can see the results of hard physical effort. We went to bed directly after supper and though the wind beat at our door and windows we were able to rest. We knew our own dogs were snug and warm and even if neighboring dogs broke free, there would be little likelihood of their wandering on such a night.

Sometime in the early morning hours, the snow turned to sleet and then rain. We were almost afraid to look out in the morning for fear all the snow would be washed away, but it wasn't. The rain and sleet had merely put a glaze on and then, in the afternoon, the wind shifted from east to west and the blizzard started in again. I noticed because I was typing by the west window and suddenly found myself

in a shower of snow. It was blowing through out vent hole
—a situation we promptly remedied with a plug made from
the leg off a suit of discarded long underwear.

Also with the change of wind direction, our walls began
to break out with patches of moisture. At first we could not
figure why but at length decided they marked breaks in the
insulation of the sod walls caused by the tunnels of field
mice. The mice, we had found, did not hibernate and when
two or more did happen to find their way inside the cabin
they seemed as noisy as a herd of buffalo—especially in the
still of the night.

No plane came with mail that day. I started out for the
Trading Post to get some extra supplies and found the terrain totally unfamiliar. The wind made a whirling white
smoke screen of ground snow completely camouflaging the
lie of the land. There was no horizon, no identifying land-
mark—only a gray, numbing nothingness. Old drifts were
growing larger, new drifts were forming and these divided
the village like parallel dikes. I lost my equilibrium completely, stepping high for drifts that weren't there and
falling flat into drifts I could not see and didn't expect. It
was dangerous and extremely disagreeable walking, and so
I returned to the cabin.

That night we were to have gone to the Sewing Society
auction but when the wind changed to east again after supper and became even more violent, we decided to stay in.
Again we gave ourselves over to the fundamental satisfaction of having done battle with the storm and won—at
least temporarily—the spoils of comfort. In a victorious
mood, I made a batch of fudge and we stayed up far beyond our usual bedtime to read through a stack of magazines
some friends had sent to us on the last plane.

"I think I'll check the dogs," Fred announced as we prepared to turn in.

He stepped into the outer room and—into a mound of snow. Though we had covered the cracks in the door after shoveling out that day, the snow was now blowing from underneath and above and there was even a little drift from the keyhole.

Seegoo was again sitting forlornly outside his house. Despite the sack over the entrance, the inside was again filled with hard-packed snow. His chain was so shortened he might have been completely buried, had Fred not gone out when he did.

We decided Seegoo should spend the night inside with us and a happier decision for him we could not have thought up. While Fred went to check the rest of the team and the puppies, I watched Seegoo revel in luxury he had all but forgotten. First he took measure of the turn of events in a deliberate and prolonged stretch to his full growth. Then, as no command came to dispel the dream, he began to make himself at home.

He sniffed. Every inch of the floor. And as high as his nose could reach on the wall. Finally, deciding the situation really was true as well as good, he turned to me and with a gentle nuzzle informed me some petting was in order. Obligingly (for I had missed petting him) I began to knead the thick mat of down along his spine and so overcome was he, he simply swooned against my knee and would have fallen to the floor had I moved from supporting him. At length, having reached satiety, he oozed to the floor and with a contented grunt, slept—in full possession of his new quarters.

But Seegoo's nirvana was short lived. Fred came in slamming the door behind him, his parka covered with snow.

"It's bad," he said. "The big dogs are all right but the puppy pen is completely filled with snow and the pups are out. You'll have to help me round them up." Then he was gone again, while I put on sweater, parka, outer drill parka, boots, wool gloves and fur mitts as quickly as I could and went out to join him.

In my haste I neglected to close the doors and this once it happened to be a good thing for I was no sooner out than the puppies rounded themselves up and charged into the cabin like the bulls of Pamplona—and yipping, feinting, lunging, fumbling all over each other made en masse for Seegoo.

Seegoo, at first bewildered, was soon tormented beyond endurance. Being too much of a gentleman to hurt the puppies, he resorted to deep-throated growls which would send them packing just long enough to reform ranks and swarm again. It was bedlam multiplied by seven.

We allowed Seegoo up on our cot—an indulgence he had never before been permitted, but even here he was not out of reach of his tormentors. They would stand on their hind legs and literally leap for a bite of fur and, upon falling back, scramble up to leap again.

We decided the situation called for extreme measures and went to Seegoo's rescue with folded newspapers. Taking stations on the edge of the bed, we flailed away at the attackers, while Seegoo once more relaxed. Only this time he relaxed even more completely for he lay on softness—soft as the fleecy clouds he might open one eye to watch on a summer afternoon. He rolled over on his back, his legs in the air, and both of us were positive he went to sleep with an open-mouthed grin on his face.

We, in turn, resigned ourselves to a night of swatting and swabbing up after our untrained guests, but this time Seegoo called the turn. The thick coat he had grown from living entirely outdoors soon made him unbearably hot. He began to gasp for breath and plead with agonized eyes to go where it was cooler.

We had one alternative and that was to put Seegoo in the outer room and this we did. Then, we thought, surely then we would get some rest. But we failed to consider the fact that though the light from the lamp was turned off, the puppies' activities were not. They continued to sniff and scuffle, to yap and to sneak potatoes out of the box under the table, to pull at the spread until we turned on the light again. As long as we were being kept awake anyhow, we decided we should watch the destruction.

With the light and with the night before us, we had a chance to study the puppies closely for the first time and to decide on their names.

We had already naturally come to call one of the male puppies Sookgah (fast one) and his all white sister Nanook (polar bear). Now we noted that except for Sookgah whose face wore the classic Malemute mask with a distinguishing black streak down his nose, the rest of the litter were all paired in markings. Nanny had a twin, another all white female and to her we gave the name of See-oo-ti. This was the Eskimo word for "ear" and that was the word chosen because among all the puppies her ears were the only ones already standing erect.

There were two with blaze faces—the other male, shaggy, good natured, broad beamed with a freckled nose and this last feature was what determined his name: Kinguk (nose). His twin became Newcah (little sister). There were two masks sporting a single lavalier of white in the center of their foreheads and these we called Mik-nik-rok (the smallest, which indeed she was) and Kah-fik (wolverine) because her coloring was exactly the same. Such distinctive paired markings we felt would make an outstanding team in appearance with Sookgah at lead, if Sookgah would turn out to be a leader.

Sookgah was the only one of the seven who was calm

enough to take petting. He was content to sit quietly in our laps while we ran our fingers through his silky down, which had, as all puppies have, the faint sweet scent of clover. The other six that evening began to wear out their welcome in a short time with their scratching and play-fighting and recurring disregard for our floor. Before an hour had passed we felt compelled to do some improvising in the outer room. We made a barrier of a chest of linens, shutting Seegoo off at one end, and turned the seven pups into the other. Then, we scoured the cabin floor and went to bed.

And all was quiet except for the raging of the blizzard.

The next morning a reverberating growl from Seegoo told us one of the pups had made the barrier. We opened the door

to numerous droppings and puddles (mercifully frozen)

to a chewed-in feed sack and scattered meal

to a linen chest with the lid open and its contents befouled and

to a shattering chorus of yaps from seven pups suddenly awake and demanding to be fed.

We lifted Sookgah out of Seegoo's section and put him back with his brother and sisters and quickly shut the door. It was a situation that could only be faced once we were fortified with food and dressed for shoveling.

When we had finished breakfast and went out the snow was coming in horizontal gusts and the wind cut through our fur parkas. We looked at the thermometer on our window sill, which we hadn't been able to see from the inside because of the frost, and found it registering eight below.

Again we shoveled all day, first Seegoo's house and then the puppy pen and after that all the other dog houses, which though not snowed under entirely were effectively blocked. Our west window was completely buried again along with the entire west end of the cabin. We tried then to figure out what obstructions were causing the drifts to form where they did since the blizzard gave no promise of letting up. We moved part of a stack of wood near Seegoo's house and hoped that would affect the direction of snow.

And the blizzard continued its onslaught.

On the third morning we slept "long" and when we did get up it was with a vague feeling of something wrong. At first we could not think what it was and then we realized. The quiet. The utter quiet. There were no sounds of the village stirring about—of wood splitting or dog howls. We raised the shades and there was nothing because both windows were snowed in. When we opened the outside door it was on a world of white, and hush. Only here and there smoke rose straight up from a mass of white the shape of a house. Having met the blizzard the villagers were sleeping off their exhaustion.

Everywhere there were drifts. A monstrous drift in front of the Trading Post, a perfectly formed, match-sized drift in the wake of a blade of grass. In places the snow was flush with the entrances to the caches. Outhouses were completely buried, nor would the snow over paths leading to them be disturbed until spring. The "sanitary aid" now being several feet beneath the new surface of white, sewage disposal would be largely in frozen heaps on the ground. There would be no more garbage collections, for the cans were buried, too.

The dogs were deep inside their snow-plastered houses but whether it was because we had altered the course of the drifts or the fact that the wind had changed direction during the night, neither Seegoo's house nor the puppy pen were snowed under.

Gradually the village began to stir.

We saw Gene digging out his dog houses and Fred went

to fill two five-gallon buckets with snow and called to him, "We finally got our snow."

"Yes. Have to take shovel in cabin at night to dig way out," Gene answered. He watched Fred shoveling from a bank. "What you do?"

"Getting some snow for dog water. It'll be a lot easier than getting ice."

Gene walked over. "That snow make your dogs poor. It have salt in it."

"Salt? Where from?"

Gene shrugged, "Don't know. Nobody ever give it to dogs. It make them poor."

"Well, thanks, Gene," Fred told him. "I'll test it."

He brought the buckets in and set them to melt on the little stove. We boiled a sample and could detect no salt and so started giving the dogs snow water from then on, with periodic taste tests. Only once did we find a trace of salt. It was after a west wind which led us to think perhaps salt had worked to the top of the sea ice and been blown inland. Even then we found that beneath the top crust the snow was pure as always. Our dogs remained in prime condition on snow water, yet none of the villagers that we knew of would try it simply because none had for generations. The result was their dogs sometimes did not have water, while ours always had plenty.

With the snow, the best time of year began for the sled dogs.

Once the village was awake, team after team was hitched and driven across the slough and the first portage and on upriver for ice. With every joyful streaking through, all the other teams would set up a frantic cry to go along. We decided the time had come for Seegoo to "fulfill his destiny."

We went over to see Alec just as he was returning from a

trip upriver and asked if he would harness Seegoo with his team for a short trial run. We reasoned his dogs might be a little subdued and our neophyte thereby better able to keep up with them. Alec was happy to oblige but he did not think we should put Seegoo in front as his leader might resent it, rather at the back position of "wheel" next to the sled.

Alec's team watched the harnessing with arched backs and ruffled hair. The two immediately in front of Seegoo turned half-way to face him and literally went up on tiptoe daring him to start something. Our "Beeg Dog," on the other hand, took it as a great and glorious game, pushing his face practically in their open mouths while doing semaphore signals with his tail.

When Alec gave the signal to go, his dogs leaped forward as sure, straight and swift as a thrust harpoon. With the initial wrench Seegoo looked as startled as a dog could look, slid along on his chin some fifteen feet then, of necessity, broke into an uneven, awkward gallop. Every few minutes he would look back at us and bark elatedly, not getting an idea at all that running in harness was serious business. On the return trip he tired. His tugline was slack and he let the other dogs pull him. But he did not lie down or balk as many dogs did the first time in harness and Alec told us he should make a good sled dog though he did not know about a leader.

In the days that followed, we had ample opportunity to find out.

There were trips upriver for ice. The second time, we persuaded Alec to harness Seegoo beside the leader and when he did a surprising instance of canine psychology resulted. The leader, Sport, instead of challenging the upstart in a fight as we had expected, simply collapsed into an ineffectual mass of hurt feelings and bewilderment. He refused to sniff or even look at his new running mate. When Alec gave the signal to go, Sport cowered and slunk until the two dogs behind him were running abreast of his hind legs. It wasn't that Sport lacked spirit for he had always shown a fine leadership when out with Alec and the team. It was more that he had always done his best and he could not understand why Alec should train another leader. Alec finally unharnessed him and told us to go on and started leading him off. We called to Seegoo to "gih" (go).

He looked around eager-eyed, ears up and started circling to the back of the sled.

"No, Seegoo," we said, "gih," and pointed the way time and time again. But each time his reaction was the same. Seegoo could not understand why we did not want him to come to us as always before. Fred went up to trot beside him and the rest of the dogs fell in and as they did we heard as heartbroken a wail as any sled dog ever made. From the bank, Sport had seen his team going off with another leader and it was all Alec could do to hold him.

With Fred trotting beside Seegoo we followed the newly broken trail upriver. Several times we passed dog teams returning and several times dog teams passed us going up. We gave them a wide berth. We did not want any dog fights, for we felt Seegoo would be massacred, nor did we want the other dogs hurt.

We found our ice stacked just where we had left it and luckily the tide had not affected it. The ice was so thick it could no longer be sawed in neat blocks but had to be hacked out with a pick. Even though we were dressed completely in furs, the cold was undeniable. When we slid ice across the frozen river, it had the sound of broken crockery, it was so brittle. Before we were finished the moon came up silverplating the snow and making exquisite highlights on the sculptures of the wind. In this pristine loveliness we made the return trip.

Seegoo loped joyously beside Fred and though he still didn't get the idea at all, he presented a nice picture, tail held high in a spirited lope. Fred, however, was beginning to tire of being co-lead dog.

"You just wait, Old Boy," he muttered. "You'll find out life is made of sterner stuff."

Seegoo had his first small taste of "sterner stuff" only moments later when we ran into overflow where the ice had cracked and water seeped through. Although there might be danger of freezing from a wetting in overflow or even drowning, this was only inches deep. We did take the standard precaution of running the dogs through loose dry snow to dry their paws so ice wouldn't form between the pads. We hoped Seegoo would learn a lesson from this—to go around water or if not that, then through it cautiously. And to bite off ice between his pads, should it form.

Fred stopped by Alec's to leave his dogs and I walked home across the spit. When I saw Seegoo alone pulling Fred and the sled toward the cabin, I gave a call. Seegoo lunged forward and straining in his harness raced towards me, while Fred clung to the handle and rode the brake. Our faithful pet would come to us as always but was not yet ready to go away from us.

By moonlight we read our thermometer and were not surprised to see the mercury sitting on minus fifteen.

Photography in such weather ranged from frustrating to agonizing. The maximum hours of light for shooting were limited to around four. The cold took our energy and so did the mere physical effort of putting on extra clothes and taking them off several times a day. Added to it all was the trial of getting our main character, Seegoo, to enact the part of leader.

We had counted on Seegoo learning his role while running beside Alec's leader. But Sport's refusal to cooperate had nullified that plan. Since Sport wouldn't be used, there was no point in hiring the rest of Alec's team and so we started running Seegoo with our own four dogs, none of whom had ever been a leader.

Fred continued the training by trotting beside Seegoo every step, now with a lead line to teach him "Gee" and "Haw." There were regular sessions since it was necessary to use the dogs every day—to go upriver for ice; or up the coast for "dry" wood; or out on the sea ice to dump our garbage and frozen sewage; or for photography.

By now the Bering Sea was frozen for several miles out and smooth as a marble counter. One afternoon, however, we found the surface cracked in many places and vapor issuing as if from fumaroles. With hands clumsy in woolen undergloves (necessary to prevent "burning" flesh on the metal) we set about photographing this phenomenon of cold. We had to work quickly and make the first "take" do, for our cameras, even though professionally winterized, still slowed to a stop just after one reel. Since this would necessitate a long and gradual thawing out back at the cabin to prevent fogging, we decided to spend the rest of the afternoon in training Seegoo.

I stood on the runners at the back of the sled while Fred ran alongside. As soon as he felt Seegoo was getting into the lope, Fred would let the team pass and then leap into the sled. But each time as Seegoo sensed he was running alone he would look over his shoulder and upon seeing us, start back. The training became even more frustrating than the photography. For Seegoo, too. He simply could not comprehend why we didn't welcome his coming with praise and a pat.

"I just don't think he has what it takes," Fred declared wearily. "Let's try one of the other dogs."

Feeling deep disappointment in Seegoo for the first time in the four years we had owned him, we led him to the back of the team and harnessed him next to the sled at the position of wheel.

Then we put Lynx—the spirited one, the would be fighter, the next largest to Seegoo—in the lead spot.

Fred took over the driving while I settled in the sled expecting a good ride. Lynx had run for several years in a team and should know to go forward if not the command of "Gee" or "Haw."

"All right," Fred called out and then "Gih."

Nothing happened.

Fred repeated the command.

Lynx did not budge. Finally he sat down and then he lay down and there was no getting him up. We ordered, we cajoled, we threatened. Fred even fastened a leadline on his collar and pulled but none of this had the slightest effect. Lynx being lazy by nature did not want the job of setting a pace. He preferred to slouch along with as slack a line as he possibly could. We realized we had made a poor decision and put him back. We studied over the three remaining dogs and selected Brandy, the singer, because he had been one of Alec's best pullers.

To our complete astonishment, he would have none of being at the head of the team either. He did not lie down but he would not go forward. He just stood, tail dragging, cowed like an animal bearing the brunt of a storm and so we put him back in his spot and brought Arbo, the gentleman, forward. Gentle though he was, we hoped perhaps he would assert a quiet leadership but—he wouldn't. He remained rooted just as Brandy had done. No matter how we coaxed or tugged, he did not want the responsibility of leading.

That left Ot-key-luk (no name), the pup. Surely this one would have a spirit to go.

But Ot-key-luk's performance was no more impressive than the others. The only spirit he showed was to go back to run beside Brandy again. We appeared to be back exactly where we had started. All the shifting about had produced no different spirit whatsoever in any of the dogs with one exception—Seegoo.

Seegoo had reacted noticeably to each change for as Fred tried each dog at lead, Seegoo would leap forward straining against his harness to get ahead. Not only when we were calling encouragement or gave the signal to go, but every moment. Seegoo plainly did not want to run behind the other dogs. We noted his increasingly frantic efforts to get ahead and a realization began to form. Perhaps being demoted had been a lesson.

We put Seegoo back at lead and with one mighty lunge he thrust forward pulling and pulling as he had never pulled before. Fred let Seegoo and the team pass him and boarded the sled and Seegoo kept going forward. He did not know to go to the right or the left but he did know that he wanted to keep ahead of the rest of the dogs. They, in turn, were fully content to have him take over. They fell in behind him and soon even Seegoo lapsed into the regular lope of veteran sled dogs. We began that day to have the first hope that in Seegoo might lie the makings of a leader.

CHAPTER

9

Seegoo began to act like a sled dog in other ways.

When we would bring the tow line and harnesses out from the "porch" he would go into a howling frenzy with the rest of the team. And now—he knew what he was howling about. If other teams ran down the main path, Seegoo strained at his chain and leaping like a seesaw, first on his hind legs, then on his front, demanded to go too. He even joined in the baying chorus of the other dogs at night, though his attempts were thin and quavery and hardly sled-doglike in sound.

Except when the wind was blowing he stayed outside his house and as a result developed a magnificent coat which gave all the protection he needed. We noticed another characteristic developing. That of ownership. Seegoo had always been a fastidious eater, pecking dainty bites of food, walking away to take a drink of water, returning to his pan again over a length of time. But now, with other dogs around, there was no trifling. If a puppy happened to escape and come near Seegoo while he was eating, we would hear a growl that was an unmistakable warning.

Once winter was upon us, we started giving our dogs warm water. We mixed the puppies' meal with warmed water too, since Dave told us they would be teething and need soft food for a while. The vapor from it would frost their fur and turn their whiskers to ice and this quick freezing of steam provided a favorite trick for the children of the village. Jutting out their lower jaw, they would breathe furiously until their eyebrows and forelocks and parka ruffs were all covered with frost. It gave them an appearance of being pre-prematurely gray.

With the snow, the children started playing a game called "King of the Mountain." The girls would climb the large snowdrift in front of the Trading Post and then the boys would charge and pull them off.

When they were all pulled off, it was the boys' turn to be the "Kings of the Mountain" and subject themselves to an onslaught from the girls.

Sarah continued to come every afternoon. There would be a slight tap at the door and once inside she would lean against it catching her breath. She and many of the young girls had to run to keep warm when going about the village because they would not wear fur boots or parkas instead of their mail-order clothing. As soon as she could talk, she would deliver her "news."

"So and so have birthday." "So and so have new baby."

She was to speak a "piece" at the mission Christmas program. She was going to give hers with others but some gave them alone. Mama had cut her braids off for the program, that being the reason she refused to take her head scarf off for several days. Sister was going to give her a permanent.

Ruthie Otton was a constant companion and the first substitute dishwasher, except on Tuesdays, when they both had catechism classes and Fred took over.

As the days grew shorter and darker and the cold held,

Howard's appearances became more sporadic. We could not blame him. He did not have boots and we didn't like to take him out with the dogs without them. He asked if he might mop the floor for me and I agreed. This gave him work indoors and a chance to tease the girls, both of which he found to his liking. When the floor didn't need mopping, we found ourselves paying Howard to report, anyway, in the event we might want to photograph him, but he came less and less regularly.

When Howard did come and Sarah and Ruthie were there and our Number three boy too, going in and out for wood, chatter and laughter filled the one room of Mik-nik-rok to the ridge pole. In addition to what we came to call "the children's hour" there were nearly always one or more callers.

Elizabeth came with fresh blubber "good for dogs in cold weather" and a surprise for me. It was a pair of socks of rabbit fur she had made after hearing me complain of cold feet. They would have been much too small had they been of a more definite shape but, by letting them slide down on my heel, were usable and comfortable. Elizabeth took Jonathan in her lap and settled herself with graham crackers and coffee. We always passed the crackers to our helpers too, and between their listening with undivided attention to the stories of their elders and munching tiny bites, it was a long time before the dishwashing was done and the water "spilled" (poured out).

Or Thora might come as she did one day with Fred's enlarged boots.

"Mat like Eskimo (she was referring to the mat I had made) house like gussok!" Then, she started teasing Fred about the enormous size of his boots. "Maybe you think you get lost on ice . . ."

"How would big boots help me then?" Fred obliged her by asking.

Before she answered she took the cup of coffee and graham crackers we offered and settled herself on the floor, legs outstretched. Then she began her story.

"Three mens get lost on ice once. Two laughed at the other's big muh-mee-luks without any shape. Then it get cold. Colder and colder. Then mens not laugh any more. Man with big muh-mee-luks just reach down in boot and change grass around. Not have to take boot off."

I went to get the grass Elizabeth had given me for lining our boots and asked Thora how to arrange it. Deftly she took a handful and made a figure eight with it that took the pressure off the heel and ball of the foot and would not alter too much with wearing. This would go underneath the felt insole we used as liners.

"When I was a little girl, I didn't wear socks," she reminisced. "My grandmother have me stand on grass. Then she fold part over this side (she made a motion over the right side of her foot) a part over the other side and the middle down over the toes. Then the heel up. It stay there. It keep foot warm."

We gave Thora a new sewing assignment—to make a squirrel-skin parka liner to be worn inside my seal-skin parka. There were not enough skins around Unalakleet since most of the women no longer trapped, so it would be necessary to purchase them from the trader at Shaktoolik at 60 cents per skin, plus 20 cents for tanning. As she had done for the boots, Thora measured entirely with her hand and fingers. She counted the number of fingers across the front and the space between the yoke and the underarm was the length between the outstretched forearm and finger. The distance between the elbow and the thumb was the height of the parka hood from the shoulder.

When she rose to go we urged her to take an armful of canned goods from our shelves.

"I wish I had trouts," she exclaimed.

"They have them at the Trading Post," I told her.

She wrinkled her nose. "I not like them, I like last year's. I like them fermented with guts in. Guts give kick." She turned to Elizabeth, "You have?"

Elizabeth shook her head.

"You see. That Eskimo way," Thora explained. "If I ask, it all right I get turned down."

I asked her how she was coming along on the boot order. For a moment she was uncomprehending and then remembrance came. "Oh, you mean for store outside?"

"Yes."

"I not work on them for a while," she said. "Making boots for Christmas now."

Already the villagers were full of talk and plans for Christmas and our own Mik-nik-rok began to assume a holiday air as we decorated our gables with Christmas cards and strung them along the ridge pole. New additions were noted by our youth corps each day, minutely examined and evaluated to determine which they liked "best of all."

Our extra Christmas seals and stickers we used to border our windows and wall and the effect proved so pleasing on the drab kraft paper, we left them there the rest of our stay. Packages began to arrive from the States plus the mail orders we had placed ourselves, all adding to the general clutter of Christmas ribbons and wrapping paper.

Sarah was in an agony of curiosity when she learned that her present from us was in the sea chest not four feet away from where she washed dishes.

Elizabeth reported that Postmaster Frank Ryan had telephoned Santa Claus for Jonathan—a courtesy he performed over the line connecting the Trading Post with FAA.

Iris launched the season's festivities with a "coffee" at the clinic. She had issued invitations in "shifts" as was the general custom, but when we came in on the third shift we were offered seats by the first persons to rise and leave from the first shift.

This was followed by a second "coffee" at FAA and close upon that was the Mother's Club auction. Among the items successfully bid for was a string of popcorn for $1.25 which we would use to decorate our Christmas tree and a three-layered cake going to the Postmaster's wife for $7.00. The cake, naturally, was cause for another party the next evening at the Postmaster's.

At this affair the two dozen guests sat in two rows of facing chairs. The room where the party was held was large having been built to serve as accommodation for visitors in the village. There was ample space for Sarah's father to start the fun with a native dance which he did—stamping and chanting back and forth the length of the room.

Then, with dramatic gestures and inflection, Frank told of a race he had run and won many years ago.

The story which took the prize for physical prowess, however, was that of a grandmother who related with just a hint of pride how she had used to breast-feed her baby without bothering to take him from her back.

The Russells had bought a Christmas tree at the auction. It was their fourth tree, the first three having been so brittle from cold when felled, they arrived skeletons. The one they had bid on and won looked fairly plump—an effect achieved by the wiring on of additional branches. We spent an evening helping Lillian and Floyd decorate their house and the "poor cripple" and that put us in a mood to go for ours.

The next morning, with the thermometer at ten below, we hitched the dogs. They were so excited about going we only attached the lines to their collars, leaving their tuglines go, except on Seegoo, until they had worked off some surplus energy. The sled screaked and skimmed over the powder dry snow which showed cracks here and there where the ground had split open from the cold. We followed the trail north along the coast for several miles and then, when we began to see trees, struck out across the tundra. The going was rough—uneven with clumps of grass and the snow deep, and here Seegoo proved his worth, never faltering, plunging up to his chest, sometimes pulling the other dogs through. Fred had to put on his snowshoes to pick out a trail, while I rode the runners at the back.

The selection, or rather hunting out, of our tree took a much longer time than we expected. Primarily we wanted a full one and the limitations of Mik-nik-rok prescribed it must be short. We had no trouble whatsoever meeting the second requirement but a well filled out tree wasn't to be found. We finally selected three. One we used as a cushion in the sled for the second tree, and the third I held upright in my arms all the way back. We couldn't help but think what a float we would have made in any large city parade.

Once home we combined two of the trees into one. Then, using our small tripod for a stand, we gave it a place of honor on our clothes chest, though it had to be moved whenever we wanted to take clothing out or had company. The third tree we ceremoniously thrust into the snow beside Seegoo's house and after his four months' stay on a barren sandspit, it was a question whether Seegoo or we enjoyed the tree more.

In the evenings at Mik-nik-rok, we made our Christmas tree decorations—chains of bright Christmas paper, icicles out of tin strips peeled off coffee cans, strings of cranberries flown in from Anchorage, snow balls from marshmallows and for the top, a silver star whose gleaming foil once held a pound of tea.

Two nights before Christmas, Fred put on a spotlessly white parka cover and I my new boots and off to the mission program we went. This was unquestionably *the* event of the season for the villagers but this year in addition to the excitement of the program was the long looked-forward-to opening of the new mission. For many months it had been under construction, the framing and exterior work being done in warm weather and the interior finishing during the cold months. Now the last sanding of the knotty pine interior was done, the ends of the pews were a gleaming white, the sills around the amber-stained windows had been brought to a satin-smooth sheen. The villagers along with Reverend Londborg and volunteer worker Spencer Strand, who had come all the way from New England to help, had done an inspired job. The mission with its simple lines, natural wood exterior and graceful spire was one of the loveliest in all Alaska.

This evening it was to be used for the first time. It smelled new and clean and was a shining bright setting for the shining bright youngsters who got up to say their "piece." All of the performers had on at least one new article of clothing—some of them entire new outfits. Theoretically, the clothes were Christmas gifts but since packages were nearly always opened as soon as received, the wearing of them beforehand was the natural thing to do. There were bright-colored hair ribbons in every little girl's black, fresh-washed hair, there were new boots, and if not these, then made-over hand me downs new to the wearer.

We picked Sarah out immediately, wearing a new long rayon dress and every hair on her head tightly curled.

The mission was packed with the children's families who

leaned forward eagerly as their own performed and whose lips moved right along with the words of the "pieces" being given. It was a trying week for parents, with the school program the next night and the agony of watching their offspring performing all over again.

And then it was Christmas Eve.

We went to the Russells and started the evening off by taking a bath. After that came a turkey dinner and the opening of our presents—except for our gift to Floyd, which hadn't arrived. It was near twelve when we stepped out into the Night Before Christmas, next door to Santa Claus.

Immediately we knew it to be one of our coldest nights for we felt a pinching in our nostrils as the moisture on the hairs began to freeze and pull. When we looked up, it was as if we saw the heavens through a magnifying glass, the stars were so close and luminous, while underfoot, the snow had the metallic sound of a fine steel band being flexed.

All through the village the beams of flashlights traced bearers of Christmas gifts and greetings. There was a certain etiquette to the use of flashlights. If we met someone on the way and they spoke, we did not shine the light in their faces but held it aside and asked "who?" We did this after we noticed everyone showing the same consideration.

We found Mik-nik-rok inhospitably cold but with a hand heavy on the fuel-oil can, comfort was soon established. We invited Seegoo in to spend the evening with us and then we began opening gifts under our skinny little tree. From Fred there were the squirrel skins for my new parka liner and a birch basket made by a native from a village farther north. My gifts to him were a pair of sealskin work mittens with a "pointer"—the index finger stitched separately—and a fur cap.

During the afternoon, friends had streamed in to "present" us. The word "present" being pronounced as a noun but quite appropriately used as a verb. And now we turned to these. There were berries and canned garden vegetables, hand-embroidered pillow cases, handkerchiefs, a calendar from the mission, canned moose and dried fish. From Alec, there was a pair of lovely pottery ducks and from Sarah— Sarah "present" Fred with a fancy white apron with "Tuesday" embroidered on it to remind him of his dishwashing chore on the day she had catechism.

Most of our friends and kin on the mainland sent food stuffs, enabling us to enjoy such unlikely combinations as hearts of palm and seal liver and rum babas and reindeer tongue in the weeks to come. There was even a can of meat for Seegoo. We made a ceremony of opening each package and never had wrappings seemed so artistic, nor gifts so thoughtfully chosen.

When it was very late we took Seegoo out to the comfort of 40 odd below and let our fire go down and as it did we toasted each other a Merry Christmas and crawled into our sleeping bag. We lay there savoring its soft warmth, smelling the "down on the farm" odor of our darkened kerosene lamp and then we heard it—faint and far away but ineffably sweet—a chorus of beloved, familiar Christmas carols. Slowly, slowly the music came closer as the carollers made their way through the village, stopping often to finish a number before going on. Now they were outside our own Mik-nik-rok giving full-throated harmony to the best known carol of all "Silent Night, Holy Night." There was a pause, a shouted "Merry Christmas!" and they were off to the next house. This was but the first of several groups who all that bitter cold night rejoiced in song the birth of their Saviour and who made the meaning of Christmas omnipresent in the village.

Christmas morning we awoke to a sound like meal being rattled in a box. We thought Number three boy must be in the outer room getting dog food until we realized it was Seegoo's chain dragging across snow so dry and brittle it echoed a rattle.

Such a morning invited us to burrow deep into our sleeping bag but it was a luxury that did not tempt us for now was our time to pleasure in Christmas.

We hurried through breakfast and immediately our fun began with the transferring of many packages from a large box into our packboards. There were small packages and large ones, soft ones and hard ones and all were gaily done up in different colored ribbons and wrappings. Some were round like balls and some were flat as picture books, some were the shape of tin horns and others of dolls but all—all were toys such as a child might awake to find in his stocking on Christmas morning. When we had first opened the assortment the night before we had thought it a mistake—that we were recipients of gifts intended for a children's home. But after going through the entire contents, the realization had come that here was the most inspired gift of all our gifts —the gift of giving to others. We had carefully rewrapped each toy and now to them we added fruits and vegetables and meats we had ordered by air from Anchorage for Christmas dinners. Then, upholstering ourselves with layers of clothing, we shouldered our packboards and stepped into the 38-below morning.

"Merry Christmas!" it was Howard jumping up from behind the first snowdrift. He told us he had come to show us the fine new boots he was wearing but we rather suspected he had dropped by to pick up his present of socks and a fountain pen, too.

After "presenting" Howard, we went to Elizabeth's to admire her tree so cleverly contrived we could not tell where branches had been wired on. Clever decorations too—a few from the mail-order house but most by her own ingenuity, like bright colored bottle caps and cutouts from Christmas cards. There was not a toy in sight. Nor a gift. Nor wrapping paper. This proved to be true in all the homes we visited except one and we went wherever there were children. We could not understand it. Packages had been arriving through the mail for weeks. We knew some had been opened immediately, but had all? Had the gifts been exchanged late Christmas Eve or early Christmas morning and put away? If they were put away was it to avoid hurt feelings or envy? Or were they out of sight because by ancient custom a poorer caller might rightfully claim a share of the wealth? We never found out. It was in Alec's home alone that toys were spread over the floor and the children enjoying them.

Next to call on Old Time friends—Thora, Dave, Marian, Accebuck, Stephan—and then, to the mission home to leave a miniature church with an electric light.

Another reaction intrigued us and that was the manner in which our gifts were received. They were accepted as if they were something due. Sometimes we received a diffident "Coo-yah-nah" (thank you) more often, not. Alec's easy and sincere thanks was an exception and, of course, the missionary's.

Sarah and Ruthie and two other friends were waiting for us when we returned from our calls. All wore new fur boots, though we never saw Sarah wear hers again after Christmas day. For a little girl who, upon learning of the arrival of her Christmas present almost two weeks before, had told us in all seriousness, "Mrs. Machetanz, I *can't* wait," she had done very well. Now, with the waiting at an end, she did not even remove the paper from the package but put it aside to take home and open.

She told us of all the gifts everyone had received and then, "Frank Ryan give me a box of chocolate."

"How nice."

"Yes. I'm his oo-zoo-uk." This meant Sarah had been the first baby born in the village after the death of the first Mrs. Ryan. According to tradition, the spirit of the deceased entered the new-born and for this reason, Frank had a special feeling toward her.

Both Sarah and Ruthie were still struck with the wonder of Christmas and dishwashing that day was only incidental to much important conversation.

"I have news," Sarah started off. "Daisy's going to get married New Year's Eve." Daisy was her older sister. She had been my dishwasher eight years before when I had come to Unalakleet to be married. "You go to the wedding?"

"May be." I gave it the Eskimo inflection with the accent equal on both syllables. It was all I could say, because we hadn't been invited.

"You come," Sarah urged. "Anyone can come to the wedding. You just can't come to the house after if you're not invited."

"I go," Ruthie chimed in and all the others vowed they would too.

"After they marry, Ralph promise to take Daisy hunting and to pick berries," Sarah went on.

Lois, one of the visiting girls broke in, "I like to pick berries."

Yes, they all agreed they liked to pick berries.

"Is berry-picking the most fun of all?" I asked.

Yes, it was the most fun of anything.

Then, summer was the best time?

Yes, yes.

But what about Christmas?

They were all silent a minute thinking this over.

"Summer time best," Sarah decided and they all nodded.

Summer was best because of berry-picking and picnics.

"We always race picking berries," it was Ruthie.

"Oh, we do too. We do too," the others chorused.

"Papa not pick berries," Sarah took over again. "He just look." The girls all laughed, and so did we.

"Would you rather live in Unalakleet than any place else," we asked.

"Oh, I would," Ruthie exclaimed enthusiastically.

"I would too," echoed the others.

"I'm glad I'm Eskimo," Sarah said. "I'm *all* Eskimo," she added proudly.

"I am too," Ruthie declared.

"Ruthie, you are not," Sarah corrected. "Are you all white, Mrs. Machetanz?" they asked. At first I wasn't sure what they meant but concluded they were asking if I had native blood.

I told them no.

"I'm glad I'm all Eskimo," Sarah repeated. We didn't know whether she was being defensive or not, but if she wasn't we were glad, for there seemed to be so little native pride except at special times. Special times when Eskimo challenged Eskimo in old time contests of physical strength and skill.

New Year's Day was one of these times. . . .

CHAPTER

10

New Year's Day began cold and blowing snow but that did not prevent the villagers from celebrating in much the same way they had for generations.

First of the events scheduled were the dog races but long before time for them to start, the villagers began to converge on the square. The grayness of the morning they defied with bright new Christmas scarves and parka covers.

Impatiently they waited—mothers rocking from side to side to lull the babies on their backs, men stomping their feet and moving about to keep warm, ruddy cheeked children playing tag in an excess of energy. Into this panoply of swirling color came the teams. As they did, the dogs already on the scene would set up a frenzied chorus and leap into the air in uncontrollable excitement with each outburst of howling and barking generating another and another. Three men it took to hold each team, one on the brake and two up front and though the sharp commands of the drivers could be heard above the dogs, they only served to increase the pandemonium. Added to all were the delighted shrieks of the children as they darted between favored teams or drivers, intermingled with the urgent entreaties of mothers to stay back and be careful.

We watched the teams gather and though they displayed an insatiable urge to run, we were struck with the deterioration of individual dogs. Through careless breeding, some had lost their broad chests to the narrow conformation of a setter. Some had been so interbred, they were extremely nervous in contrast to the placid disposition of the true Malemute. Others, it was plain to see, had not been fed and watered enough. We decided that we had started our documentary of the sled dog not a moment too soon. Judging from teams in Unalakleet, the breed would soon be passing from the Alaskan scene except for kennel or racing stock.

Somehow in the uproar lots were drawn for starting positions and since teams were to be individually timed for the course, the first musher out was allowed a reasonable edge to break trail.

The starting signal was given and the first team was off—streaking down the main path and up the snow banks so swiftly the sled literally took to the air at the crest to land with a bang on the other side, while already the dogs were starting up the next drift.

A contrast to the confusion before the first team was off, was the reaction of the villagers to the actual racing. No cheers, no handclaps were heard to spur the drivers on. The only visible interest was a minimum turning of the head as the teams passed by. And the same was true when the teams came back. There was an occasional grunt to acknowledge the arrival of a winner, and by the time the last team was in the crowds had dispersed and the children's interest turned to other things.

The change in the dogs was just as marked. Their pace was now a subdued trot and instead of eager howls and barks, tongues were hanging out and breath came in labored panting.

Besides team races, there were obedience trials. Here the single leaders followed commands of their master's, who were not allowed to direct in any way other than the spoken word. As in years past, we marveled at the eager intelligence of sled team leaders, but at the same time were saddened to note how few dogs were well trained enough to enter this event. The outward reception of the villagers to these trials ranged from concealed interest to indifference. The majority were so little concerned with the care of dogs anymore, there was a natural disinterest in performance.

Much more spectator spirit was shown during the contests held in the National Guard hut that afternoon. Though the men remained expressionless, the women would smile and at times the children laughed out loud.

"Finger Pull" was a favorite contest indulged in from small children to old men. In this, two contestants sat facing on the floor, middle fingers of their right hands interlocked, bracing themselves with their left hands against the right knee of their opponent. The object was to pull until one or the other's finger gave.

The first man to step into the ring of spectators was John Auliye, one of the finest hunters in the village, a true old-time Eskimo who took pride in the strength that enabled him to live as his ancestors had before him.

John's challenge was accepted and the two men took their places. In a few minutes John outpulled him and the two that followed. The sure brown hands that still seined the cold waters for salmon and thrust the harpoon were stronger than the hands of men of fewer years who no longer cared to hunt and fish.

And then, Alec stepped forward and as he did a murmur filled the room. Here would be a good show. A contest between good friends and trailmates, for many were the hunts John and Alec had gone on together and great the hunting knowledge the younger had gained from the older. This would be a contest between the old and the new; John was a traditionalist and Alec was a rebel; still, each could not help but admire the man in the other.

The two seated themselves, Alec smiling, John inscrutable. Locking glances as well as fingers, they began the contest. They pulled with their muscles tensed to board-hardness, their foreheads oozed sweat, yet neither let go or gave the slightest. They pulled so steadily and with such strength, they literally raised one another from the floor and thus locked together rolled around like a bent hoop. And the sound they made—the thud of flesh hitting floor—was the only sound in that crowded room as every eye followed the bout.

At times Fred and I could hardly bear the tension. We had never witnessed such deadly competition, yet no spectator cheered or offered any audible support.

John lost.

With no more than the relaxing of one finger he acknowledged the younger man—the antithesis of his way of living —the victor and stepped stony-faced from the ring. From the audience there was a scattered smattering of handclaps but Fred and I were limp in our seats—stunned, wrenched. We felt certain those around us had been equally affected by the rivalry we had witnessed. It was just not in their nature to show it.

John may or may not have deserved his defeat. With no elimination bouts he had had to stand off all comers and this was an impossible thing to do. Just as he went down, so did Alec, though Alec good naturedly congratulated his victor when he left the ring.

But back came Alec again a few rounds later for another

try and this time he again came out the winner, only to declare hotly his opponent had not tried. Everyone else could see what Alec said was true still the loser felt, as did all the onlookers, that Alec deserved to win and so he was judged champion even over his objections.

Here was one who had left the way of his ancestors yet who remained a favorite among his people. Some of the villagers no doubt had been impressed by the status Alec had gained through hard work and careful planning, but others there were who took his winning of the finger pull as the greatest mark of his leadership.

Next came the women's finger pull and these were far less strenuous. Decorously, the contestants kept their knees covered with their parkas and there was no rolling around or sweat. Though very few tried, the ones that did were serious about it and took a real pride in their strength. It looked so easy and such fun I decided to try it. When I stepped forward Gertie Auliye—John's wife—was in the ring. She smiled indulgently but as I put out my hand instead of interlocking fingers, she grabbed my wrist and held it up.

"Ha!" she cried in mock scorn, "what she think she do with this?"

Everyone roared and so did I. Beside her rounded smoothly muscled forearm, my wrist looked puny as the neck of a plucked duck.

She locked her finger around mine and—then and there the contest ended. So powerful a purchase had she, I could not even bend my finger to pull. She quickly let go when she saw the situation. Then she grabbed my wrist again. "It take good pictures," she said eagerly, and we laughed along with everyone else.

There was other evidence of good sportsmanship.

When the woman who stood everyone off was beginning

to tire, a former winner was urged to challenge. "Let her win," she said, "she deserves it."

Even the children pulled with intense seriousness but watching them, the onlookers relaxed and smiled. Their children were always the lightness of their lives.

Some of the events were incredible feats of strength. In one, a man would lie on his back, arms stretched above his head. A second man acting as a weight locked himself around the prone man's wrists. The winner of this contest lifted the human weight up and over his head and back again six times.

The most spectacular exhibition of coordination was the last event of the day—the double kick. Here, a skin ball was attached to a rope and looped over a rafter. From a standing position, or taking two quick steps, the aspirant would leap into the air, kicking his legs straight out to touch the ball with his feet. If he did not land standing on both feet or if both feet did not touch the ball he was disqualified. Though we saw the man who took the event touch the ball several inches above his head it was still difficult to believe. The women made a poor showing. Sarah's mother was still strong and lithe in body and so was Ruthie's grandmother, but they were among the exceptions. Few there were who still retained the stamina of other days and other ways or the wish to test it.

It had been a rare New Year's Day—a day of a kind due to become even more rare for the time of pride in physical prowess was passing and without that there would be no contests.

Within the week another important and equally exciting event for the villagers took place. There was a village election and the faction in favor of making Unalakleet a townsite was voted in by a narrow margin. So now the controversy became more heated and the pros and cons of it the main topic of conversation.

Blizzards continued on and off. It was far from ideal photographic weather but the pups were reaching another stage we felt should be recorded photographically. We could no longer keep Sookgah—or Sooky as we had started calling him—in the pen and any time of day would find him loose and visiting Seegoo or the big dogs.

In his calling he always followed the same approach. That was, to come up wagging his tail from the ears back and present the black moist triangle that was his nose for a friendly touching. If he was rebuffed he would flop down and roll over on his back in as helpless a pose as he could assume, thus hoping to show he had no malicious intentions. Once the big dogs had sniffed him over and turned away he would leap up and prance around them not in the least discouraged by their massive indifference.

During the day if we happened to leave the doors open a crack he would literally tiptoe in after first easing the door open with his nose. Then he would sit quietly at the far end of the room and if we made no objection, inch over until he was beside us, his chin on our knee, beseeching us for a petting. When we awakened in the morning we would more often than not find him in the house vacated by Geena whom we had sent back to her owner the first week of the year. We decided the time had come to chain Sooky out and give him a house of his own. Although he was only four months old, there was a village ordinance against stray dogs and we were afraid something might happen to him.

We admitted Sooky's coming into manhood with a new "oogruk" (giant seal) skin collar. Then, after setting up our cameras, we chained him to a post. It was the first time in his life he had known unyielding restraint and for the next quarter of an hour it appeared he would go altogether ber-

serk. With heart-piercing yelps he would gallop to one end
of the chain with such force he was completely somer-
saulted only to leap up and do the same thing in the opposite direction. At length, with his strength spent, came the
realization he had met with something bigger than himself.
He backed away as far as his chain would permit and sat
and glowered at the odious post that would not give.

Gene had warned us to make the collar snug for if Sooky
learned to slip it off, there would be no holding him after
that and we had followed his advice. Gene had also said he
thought it would take three or four days of his raging and
crying at the chain before he would quiet down. So, we
went about it gradually. We released him after an hour and,
like a rocket, he went straight for the wall of the pen and
was up and over.

But by the next morning he had recovered his courage
and was out again paying his daily calls and investigating
the world at large. This time when we chained him he did
not react so violently and by the third day he had accepted
the chaining and his mother's house as his own. Thereafter,
he showed no inclination to return to the other puppies.

When we had started photographing the sequence of
Sooky being chained, the temperature was a minus 32 with
gusts of wind. Our cameras slowed and froze to a complete
stop after only ten minutes of shooting and then began the
laborious process of thawing. To prevent lens-fogging they
must be warmed gradually for up to an hour—first in the
outer room, next on the floor of the cabin and finally on the
table. After following this procedure twice, we realized that
one half of our light for the day was gone.

We decided to put up a small tent—an "ice shanty" we
had brought along for just such a time. And this we did,
taking another precious hour of our shooting time. It proved
to be wasted effort. True, it served as protection from the

wind but even with the warmth of our bodies and breath, the air inside the tent was still cold enough that the cameras froze. And so back for thawing, and by the time that was accomplished the light was gone.

The next day we tried putting the "little failure"—the kerosene heater that had proven so inadequate in our fall camping—to work and found it put out just enough heat to fog our lenses. When that happened the cameras had to be opened up and the moisture wiped away and the lenses were useless until they cleared which took several hours.

We went back to gradual thawing.

We encountered the same problems with our still photography. It was necessary to keep the cameras inside our parkas and take them out just long enough to click the shutter. The one time I tried changing film outdoors, it broke with cold.

We would stand in the ice shanty, stamping to keep feeling in our feet, blowing on our fingers, listening to the clothes which were frozen solid on Elizabeth's clothesline bang together like boards and thought recurringly of the advantages of photography in more temperate climes. To add to our frustration, the skies were a gorgeous cobalt blue while from the north a low level rose-tinted sun gilded the snow, yet with all the glorious coloring about us we were physically limited by the extreme cold to shooting perhaps forty minutes and thawing the rest of our four hour day.

Still we *did* get our pictures and that was the thing that mattered.

And then in mid-January, for some inexplicable reason, the mercury started to climb up and up and didn't stop until it reached 32 above. Suddenly we were in the middle of a thaw.

We couldn't believe it. We would walk into our porch and it was like entering a downpour as the frost on the ceiling melted. Seegoo's house which had filled with snow during the blizzard was filled with water and inside our own cabin telltale patches of damp began to erupt on the ceiling. Our floor was wet from tracking in snow and slush and the fur-soled boots were put aside for skin water boots.

With the break in the cold we took the pups in shifts for romps on the tundra.

The first time, it was Sookgah and two of his sisters, Mickey and Kahfik. The moment the sisters were lifted out of the pen and Sooky unchained, they were away like puffs of down before the wind. We tried to call them back but our calls were completely ignored as they darted between tufts of snow-covered grass in an ecstasy of discovery.

On and on they raced in a dead heat for the horizon and though we commanded and threatened, they had no ears for us. When just three tails were visible above the rolling snow and an occasional head as they bounced like gazelles after whatever struck their fancy, we decided to use tactics. We turned our backs on them and started toward the village. After all one has to be smarter than his dogs to train them, we told ourselves. We took several steps, then sneaked a look back. The puppies were just a dot against the distant white. With no further theorizing we reversed our direction and ran after them as fast as we could. Then, just as suddenly as they had taken flight, they wheeled and came toward us full speed. On one of their passes, we grabbed Sooky, and on another, Mickey. Having only one chain, we fastened a pup at either end and looking like nothing more than a Maypole dance, proceeded back to the village. Each day thereafter we took two of our seven puppies out along with Sookgah. We knew it was risky to turn them loose but their muscles needed strengthening for what lay ahead.

We began to train Sooky further. At Dave's suggestion we would take him on walks through the village, but always chained. He cut a showy figure, head up, tail up, almost dancing and all the time getting used to the pull against his neck.

Every day we would take Seegoo and the other dogs out too. Now and then we began to hope Seegoo was getting the idea of "Gee" and "Haw" but as yet his reactions were too inconsistent to be certain. We would really find out when we went winter camping.

We had hoped to go in early January but that proved to be a time of blizzards, one right after another. Then we had planned on the middle of the month but Harold Charles, who was to show us the way, had been unable to leave an ailing wife. The last week in January came. Harold's wife had recovered. Our supplies were all stacked and ready on the floor where they had been since the first of the year. Fred was in a running state of impatience and—I came down with a throat and bronchial infection.

It was decided that Harold and Fred should go on without me, taking a load of supplies a half-day in. The sky looked too stormy to start on a long trip and this would be a good breaking-in for the dogs.

They left with the sled cutting deep into the snow from the weight of supplies, snowshoes and two men. At the last moment, they took Sooky. Though he was young to follow a team, Harold, after appraising him closely, declared him developed enough to go. When Fred unchained him, Sooky seemed to know what it meant. Instead of taking off as he had done with the puppies, he charged over to Seegoo and tugged at his coat in impatience. Once the signal was given to go, Sooky dashed ahead and until I waved them out of sight, bounced before the team like a furry tumbleweed.

When the team returned that evening, Fred told me that once Sooky began to tire he had fallen back, even with Seegoo to heckle him with nipping all the way, but that Seegoo performed like a veteran. The going had been hard. Everywhere were deep drifts, so deep Harold or Fred had gone ahead of the team, stomping the snow down with snowshoes to break a trail and Harold had had trouble finding the way.

Next morning the weather was even less promising—overcast and windy and with dark storm clouds threatening from the east. We postponed camping until the skies were more favorable for photography and as it turned out the change in plans was a very good thing.

While we were eating breakfast, the villager from whom we had ordered two puppy houses and who was to convert the puppy barn into four accommodations came by to tell us he had decided to go trapping the next day. We had been expecting him to drop by for some time, but for the purpose of delivering the finished order, it having been placed the fall before and delivery promised by the first of the year. He further disclosed he had not even begun the job.

His renege put us in a predicament for the lives of the puppies were literally at stake. Even though the fence was now five boards high they continued to scale it periodically. It we made it any higher, more than likely the puppies would still get over it, but we could not! There was no alternative. Hastily finishing his meal, Fred put on his parka and went out to work with the carpenter.

In a freezing wind they hitched the dogs and hauled a sled load of lumber. Then they started on the two houses and by skipping lunch, completed them before the four-hour day was gone.

When it was quite dark, Fred came in, eyes streaming, his face one swollen welt from the rawhiding of the wind, his hands stiff from cold. He lit two gasoline lamps and went out again. By their light the puppy barn was made into a four unit apartment house. Our neighbors must have wondered at the goings on as they went to bed that night, for it was about then the men started tearing down the fence. If they had looked out their windows, they would have seen the outline of two figures seeming to wrestle a monster with sledge hammers and crow bars, while the two gasoline lamps made the eyes of the beast like yellow fire in the night. They would have no doubt thought the timing strange, but even stranger to our neighbors way of thinking would have been the fact the men chose to work in such disagreeable weather before the puppies ran away and made it necessary.

The last step in the project was the nailing of chains beside each door. Though this was only a temporary makeshift until posts could be put up, it presented a fine mathematical problem. The chains must be just long enough to prescribe an arc at each corner and yet not overlap. Much trial and error and time went into the figuring, but at length all was ready and the puppies were led to their new homes.

Then, we stepped back to watch while, one after the other, they reacted as if following a prescribed form entitled "upon moving into a new home." There was the preliminary inspection—the cautious sniffing beginning on the left of the entrance and going the entire way around. Once reassured, curiosity took over.

Two front paws were advanced into the opening and an appraisal of the entire interior taken. Finally deciding everything was as it should be, they entered, turned around several times and settled themselves.

We felt like cheering. Thus assured our puppies were taken care of, we looked forward to a long unbroken sleep but no sooner had we blown out the light, than this hope was gone. Gone with Fred's going into the dark, bitter cold night to investigate the clank of chains, the cause of yaps—

to find a renegade who had pulled loose or two puppies tangled. So it went the night long. For once, we welcomed the coming of the light so we could go for posts and fasten the puppies more securely.

With Sooky wailing in mammoth disappointment at being left behind, we directed Seegoo and the team to the coast. There we spent the morning hunting out straight and sturdy driftwood saplings. Once back with our load, we had to again resort to temporary measures for the ground was frozen hard as stone. The only way we could set the posts was to chisel holes in the snow and pour water to freeze them in place. We knew, if another unseasonable thaw came every one of our puppies would be loose and dragging a post behind him but it was the best we could do.

By the end of the week the weather had cleared. Fred and Harold decided to take another load and if the weather held to go on with it and set up a base camp. I was to remain at Mik-nik-rok for the bronchial infection had recurred and I had no strength.

Again I waved them off and watched Sookgah worrying Seegoo until the signal to go and, once that was given, streaking ahead of the team.

Then I went to bed, Fred having arranged for everything to be done for me so I could get complete rest.

One step he had taken was to add another employee to our payroll—Number five. Number five was an older and larger lad whose duties would include wood splitting and bringing in ice and cleaning up after the puppies which Number four had by now tired of.

Alec came every day to bring mail and check on how things were going and Elizabeth made daily calls, usually to bring some delicacy. The first time it was Russian pie, done by a recipe handed down from days of the Russian occupation of Alaska. It was made of cabbage, stored in her cellar since summer, and rice and King salmon she had preserved in brine and which tasted very nearly like fresh fish. She was sorry she didn't have any root of wild rhubarb for me to "keep in mouth and chew and suck on. Make your mouth dry but your throat well."

These three could have taken care of my every need, but as soon as word went round I was ill, the village came en masse to see that I was getting quiet and rest.

Mrs. Harold Charles dropped by to deliver harnesses we had ordered for the puppies and to inquire how I was. Her visit made me ashamed, for her third child was imminent and she had come out on a cold windy day and walked over slippery snow banks. We had a nice chat. She confided she did not like Unalakleet because it was too big a city. If it were not for sending her two daughters to school, she much preferred the days she had helped Harold herd reindeer. This she would rather do than go to club meetings or the Trading Post.

She did not want to accept any pay for the harnesses but I used the native dictum quoted to me, "I not ask. I not pay. I ask you to do it, you let me pay."

"But such nice Christmas presents," she murmured, not lifting her eyes. Then I understood. She was thanking us for our Christmas presents this way and she was only the first of everyone we had remembered at Christmas to try and "present" us with something during the rest of our stay. We continued to follow the dictum but it was nice to learn that our presents had not gone unappreciated after all.

Alec's wife came over with a pan of soup; and Thora; and Martha and her husband; and Gene and Accebuck; and Nick and Rod; and Stephan and Dave. By the end of the second day I was so tired I ate my evening meal in darkness to make an appearance of having gone to bed. But though I was tired to the point of exhaustion I would not have had it any other way, for the thought of our friends' kindness in coming would last much longer than the exhaustion.

The third day I was able to sit up for short stretches and watch the puppies through the window and a most absorbing pastime it was.

The four fractious ones of the litter we had put in the four-apartment house. Singly and together their sole concern was to make certain nothing happened to the other three that they didn't know about. When the three with houses of their own would sound an alarm, the four occupants of the apartment would stream out barking for all they were worth in all directions and having no idea what they were barking at.

They were constantly play-fighting—crouching like panthers to spring, then rolling over on their backs. When Number five poured their meal on the snow there would be a classic demonstration of mass hysteria with each yapping for attention and some getting so worked up they actually foamed at the mouth. One would have thought they hadn't been fed for weeks. They would dart back and forth to inspect each other's portion and make certain they had not been short rationed, then they would try to eat their neighbor's before tending to their own portion. And drink. They drank until they looked like they had swallowed a watermelon in one bite.

A tragic contrast to our healthy, rollicking pups was a team of dogs within seeing distance, whose owner had been sent to the Native Hospital with tuberculosis. Evidently no food had been stored aside nor did his wife give them any attention. They were literally starving at their posts and two had been all but buried during the last blizzards since they had no houses. They did not cry—that had been beaten out of them—they just lay in wraithlike coils and with sled dog stoicism waited for an end to their miserable lives. I noticed them the day the men left, but being unable to go see the owner, could do nothing about it.

Reverend Maynard Londborg dropped by the third morning Fred was gone. He was on his way to find out if the local bush pilot had happened to see two of the village men who had gone seal hunting and failed to return. They had only taken food for a day and no camping gear and now were two days overdue.

"And just reported?" I couldn't believe it.

Maynard nodded. "Sometimes the wives don't report, because it would be a reflection on their husbands as seal hunters. The husband probably wouldn't want her to."

He asked when Fred would be back. I said I wasn't certain—that supplies had been taken for up to a week of camping but that I had a feeling it would be today, since it was our anniversary.

And, just as I thought might happen, in the afternoon they returned. Sookgah was running free and so arrived ahead of the team and, never letting up speed, ran in circles around his chained brother and sisters lording his experiences over them. To me, he looked twice as large as when he had left and, in fact, he was. Fred told me the reason for his phenomenal spurt in growth, when he was recounting the trip.

"It was hard going. Deep snow all the way. We made it in all the way and set up a temporary camp and selected our site. But we didn't come back for the second load. That first night we built a fire in the stove (a light portable thin metal stove with a tiny oven) and it smoked to beat all. Harold thought at first it was the oil burning off the surface but when I came back into the tent from getting a load of wood, I saw flames coming out of the oven. I looked again and there was our bacon—the slab for the whole stay—on fire. And the sandwich meat and the reindeer. We threw it all out in the snow and went on working around camp and the next thing we knew Sooky had eaten about a third of it. We grabbed up what was left and put it up in a tree. Next morning after breakfast we went snowshoeing for about three hours looking over photographic possibilities and when we came back we saw Sooky looking like a stuffed sausage and found he'd gotten loose and finished off the bacon we'd left in the tent after breakfast." Fred said on the way back with a trail to follow, Sooky had immediately gone ahead of the team and led them all the way, looking back over his shoulder from time to time with a disdainful "what's the matter with you fellows?"

"He'll make a leader all right," Fred predicted.

"How did Seegoo do?"

"That was a funny thing. Through the deep snow where the pulling was the toughest he really led. He showed more spirit than any of them. When we were on the river where the trail was smooth I noticed him huffing—not snarling—but really dressing down the team. We couldn't see why— Seegoo being the peace lover he is—but there he was, growling over his shoulder most of the time. Then we realized, when we would start to turn right or left, sometimes the other dogs would short-cut and pull up even with him and he was telling them in no uncertain terms to get back in their place. He really was feeling his authority. He still has to learn "Gee" and "Haw." He knows now they mean "to turn," but he doesn't know which way. He's going to make a leader. Harold thinks so too."

I had much to tell Fred, too—counting off the callers and describing the antics of the pups and about the missing seal hunters and that the neighboring dogs were in a pitiful plight.

"Oh . . . that's a shame." He rose abruptly from the table and put on his outdoor clothing. "I'm just going to see Harold," he told me and left.

In a little while he was back. "Well, the dogs are taken care of." He sounded tired. He had bought them and then paid Harold to take them out on the ice and shoot them. It was the only thing to do. Cruelty to dogs was something neither of us could stomach and it grieved us to see instances of it in the village, our only unpleasant memory of our stay there.

That night Maynard and Lorraine Londborg came bringing with them a huge, pink-frosted angel food cake and ice cream to celebrate our anniversary. Maynard told us the bush pilot had sighted the two hunters far down the coast and that all was well.

"Did you get your camp set up?" Lorraine asked.

Fred nodded.

"Then you are ready to leave?"

"Yes," he told her. "We are only waiting for Sara to get well and Mrs. Charles to have her baby and a good stretch of weather. Otherwise we're ready to go any time."

CHAPTER

11

As could have accurately been predicted, the unpredictable continued to plague our camping plans.

While waiting for Mrs. Charles to have her baby, we took movies of Harold and Howard as father and son hitching the big team to go for wood and the puppies running loose after them. Since this was the first time the puppies had all been turned loose at once, it was a stage of development we had to document, even though we felt certain they would take off in as many directions as there were dogs. To our immense relief, they all stayed within the immediate area—probably attracted by the excitement of the big dogs being hitched. The moment the team took off they swarmed after them, darting in for flying nips, then off to chase each other or tag along behind—except for Sookgah. He went straight ahead of all and stayed there. In his mind he was no doubt leading the heroic serum run to Nome.

Fred was too tired to eat when we came in. He collapsed on the cot and when I touched his forehead I knew he had a fever. All night long he tossed and turned, too warm under our sleeping bag, though it was in the minus thirties and cold enough in the cabin to freeze water left in our drinking glasses. The next day he was acutely ill and that was a day we had a particularly heavy run of callers. Some of them had heard Fred was down and wanted to offer help and others just happened to pick that day to call. Gene who was out feeding his dogs, "saw your light" and decided to come. Some fruit and canned meat we had sent to Accebuck "set him to thinking of us so much" he rushed right over. Nick noticed our dogs back from their trip and came to find out why. Elizabeth thought of us as she was taking down clothes and dropped in. Fred could not even use our improvised emesis basin in private, and there we drew the line.

"I'm very sorry," I had to tell a priest who was flying through and called between arrival and departure, "but my husband does not like to be sick in front of people."

We had to cancel dinner with the trader and a talk before Lillian's art class. The next day Fred, though wobbly as a newborn fawn, insisted on getting up to give one of the movie lectures we had toured with throughout the States at the school. His voice was so weak in the beginning I was certain he would never finish, but he had been in show business too many years not to rally to applause. As the movie went on, he gained strength. The reaction of our audience to the movie was almost identical to our "outside" audiences. This should not have surprised us since the villagers were sophisticated movie goers with school movies, military movies, amateur movies of teachers and visitors, and commercial movies at the FAA.

Fred was recuperated by the first week in February. The weather turned clear and pefect. But the Charles baby, now several days overdue, did not put in an appearance.

Elizabeth came in with the first smelts of the year and a problem:

She wanted me to write the Welfare Department for some financial aid for the girl whom she had once been paid to care for by the Welfare Department and who had returned to the village and moved herself into the Sarren home. This added mouth to feed with no additional grocery money was causing a hardship. That part of Elizabeth's problem was easily taken care of before she left. The rest of it—the disciplining of a rebellious teen-ager over whom she had exercised no control for several years, was another matter. She could not get the girl to help her with housework or to tell where she was going when she went out or to come in by a certain time "but I did 'let' her stop smoking and swearing in my house," Elizabeth told me. That meant she had put an end to both.

Thora decided I would need the inner parka when we went camping and so hurried up the making of it and brought the finished product over when she came to dinner one evening. She had had a difficult time sewing it, for the skins were male and full of holes from fights and all of these had required patching. She had let it hang out so it would be damp and she could stretch it to fit. First she pulled the back across and then the sides so hard I marveled that the stitches held. Then she had me grasp the cuffs and cross my arms in front, after which she pulled the sleeves with all her strength. Once the stretching was done she vowed I would not need do it again unless I should "sweat it damp." Should this happen and the skins stiffen she showed me how to soften them, kneading them with one hand against the other, after which they were to be gently stretched— but not at the seams.

As I began to take it off she stayed my hands. "No, no

not that way." Then she showed me the correct way, grasping the top just behind the ruff with one hand and under the chin with the other. She explained this was why the strongest skins were used down the front and back center.

We sat down to supper, a meal I had given an extra amount of thought to, for Thora didn't have a tooth in her head. Everything had to be "gummed." The food was laid out buffet style on the sea chest "just like Eskimo used to do in Kashim," Thora approved. "Only then everything in one pot and everyone go help themselves from it." The menu turned out to be well chosen, for though Thora let her food grow cold while she reminisced and joked, she eventually dispatched an entire can of asparagus, several helpings of smelts and bread and fresh seal liver.

"This liver," she said, holding up a bit, "Nah-goo (good). I cook just like you. Fry till done. But when I boil I like inside still red and cold. Good raw too."

Strangely enough, her talking ran to tales of starvation. She told of a couple who were coming from the Yukon to Unalakleet in spring. Break-up had occurred and they had been forced to go to the heads of all the streams, so their "grub" ran out around Klikaterik.

"The man die. The woman think at first she lie down and die with him. Then she decided if their bodies were found side by side, people would think they been murdered, so she decided to go on." Here Thora paused a long time. Until I grew used to her pauses I had thought her stories finished, but now I knew she was thinking. "I *think* she placed her parka over him and take her ooloo (knife) and her basket and go on. She very weak. She come across dead dog. It rotten, but hair still on it because no wind blow it off." Here, another pause, while Fred and I both marveled to ourselves at Thora's wonderfully minute descriptions. "Womans think 'if I could only turn it over to get at the flesh underneath.' And she try. But she too weak. She couldn't turn it over. She finally cut off a piece just about the size of the end of a finger from the thigh and ate it and then she sick."

Fred and I laid down our forks.

"She got up to go on but she couldn't go far. So she thought 'I can't go farther' and lay down to die. Three womans who were down camping and out on ice to fish for tomcod came down the beach. One of them went up the bluff and saw this woman sitting on the ground. So the three went to her and when they lifted her face, they didn't recognize her because she had wasted away. They took her to their camp and put her away from their tents."

"Why did they do that, Thora?" I asked.

"So woman wouldn't have to see them eat and be tempted to eat. That would kill her. They just give her tiny, tiny piece of seal meat and she was nursed back to health." Then Thora sat back, smiled beatifically, and heaped a second round on her plate.

"Once there was a girl loved her brother too much. She went out to fish for tomcod because he was starving. She try and try to catch tomcod but no luck. So—she cut a piece of flesh from her own thigh and baited her hook and with that caught a couple of fish. Then she started back to the village to give them to her brother. On her way she saw a man coming toward her, but before he reach her he fall back dead. It was her brother." This time she sat back and looked sad. There was a longer pause than usual and so we concluded it was the end of the story. "If you fall backward, you never get up," Thora added. "If you fall forward you have a chance. Always fall forward."

Another pause.

"Would you like some smelts, Thora?" I asked.

She reached over and helped herself. "If I didn't eat

everything when I was a little girl, my mother would pinch my ear. Hard. 'You think that hurt?' she would ask. 'That nothing like pain in the stomach when hungry.' "

There were more stories.

Fred and I pushed aside our barely touched plates to listen, Thora finished off the buffet. When time came to leave and I had paid her for the inside parka, she was still thinking along eating lines.

"I'm going to buy myself some trouts," she announced.

"Oh? The Native store have then?" I lapsed into the local idiom.

"No, not *that* kind," she wrinkled her nose in distaste. "I want rotten fish caught last summer and put away with guts in them."

Perhaps our supper had not been quite the treat to Thora I had thought.

We continued to wait for the overdue Charles' baby and while we waited, our patience was tried in another way.

We had several weeks before received a letter stating that an insurance policy we carried had lapsed, because of an overdue premium. As we suspected, the notice had been forwarded from our previous address in Ohio by regular mail making it some weeks late in arriving. We had immediately written this explanation and sent our check but that apparently wasn't acceptable. We were informed Fred must have a complete physical to be reinstated. Again we wrote, this time of the impossibility of leaving our project to fly to Anchorage or Nome to see a doctor and asked for a period of grace. The reply came. No grace could be allowed. A complete physical was required. We resigned ourselves to losing the policy, not without some ill feeling toward what we considered to be an unbending attitude on the part of the insurer. Fred heard from Iris that a good friend of ours was coming through on the plane on a certain day—a good friend who happened to be a doctor of medicine. It was no accident that Fred was out to meet the plane that day.

"Hello, Fred," our doctor friend shouted from the plane. "How's everything?"

"Hello," Fred shouted back. "Not so good. I came out to tell you if you hear of any doctors headed up this way to ask them to stop off for a paid call."

"What's wrong?"

Fred explained the situation.

"Is that all?" Dr. Friend asked. "Come aboard. I'll give you a physical."

Fred climbed into the plane and followed Dr. Friend into the cockpit. It was about three minutes before takeoff. There he received a thump on the chest.

"Stick out your tongue," he was instructed. He did.

"Open and shut your eye." He did.

Dr. Friend clapped him on the back. "Fred, you're in fine shape. Just send me those papers and I'll see you get reinstated." As they made their way back down the aisle, "Finest physical specimen I've seen in a long time," the doctor repeated aloud to the other grinning occupants of the plane.

That much was simple. A bigger problem remained of getting a urine specimen to Anchorage, for that was another necessary part of being reinstated. Two times we tried shipping, only to receive word from Dr. Friend that the bottle had evidently frozen and broken enroute and nothing more than a soggy paper had arrived at his office. We enlisted the aid of Iris who supplied us with an especially thick bottle. This too broke. In desperation, Fred took a bottle packed in a small box out to the plane one day and handed it to the stewardess.

"This is a very valuable package that must be mailed in

Anchorage," he told her gravely. "Will you take care of it for me?"

"I'll be glad to," she smiled and placed the package in the pocket next to her heart. That way, the urine arrived without mishap and our policy was saved.

The cold held—nights in the minus thirties, days with the mercury inching up to ten below. The dogs showed the cold in the way they lifted their paws off the snow as if it burned when they stood in one spot too long.

In such weather we watched each other's face whenever we were out for the telltale white patches of frostbite. We had equipped ourselves with handwarmers and found them a quick solution, though not to be enclosed in a hip pocket, as I had learned after sustaining an inconvenient burn from one.

Now, as we took the big team out, it became evident that Seegoo had acquired some mushing know-how. He would leave the regular trail to pick his own, closer to a bluff or row of trees, so he would be in the lee of the wind, and we noticed him taking an extra sprint to get the team up and over banks. He no longer turned and faced the other dogs when we stopped, for he was undisputed boss and he knew it. Perhaps this knowledge had dated from the day Lynx had jumped him and, much to our surprise, had been throttled to defeat, though no blood was drawn.

We were pleased to find out that Seegoo pulled better with the sled heavily loaded than with an empty one—a "heavy loader" Harold termed him.

And then one day the mercury climbed from 16 below to 20 above and though winter was still all around, suddenly, the villagers began to do things done in spring. We saw children with gloves on playing marbles in a circle scraped in the snow. In the square there was a game of "bats," a form of baseball. Alec came in with rabbits he had bagged on a hunt with five other young men. Their system was to start at the head of a draw and run the rabbits down to the entrance which was blocked off by their dog teams. It must have been effective, for Alec alone bagged thirty-nine.

We were also enjoying whitefish which had been caught in traps set under the ice and shee fish—a rare game fish caught and flown in from the farther-north village of Kotzebue.

The frost in the outer room started melting again and our windows were completely clear for the first time in weeks. We were having what the Eskimos called "soft weather."

Marian and Thora called, dragging a huge sack behind them. They were collecting donations for coffees to be held during the Mission Spring Conference.

"You've done so much for the village we have come to tell you you don't need to give anything—" they began. I stuffed boxes of cookies and cans of fruit into the bag and Fred gave them cash as they fully expected we would.

As they went out Marian raised her eyebrows and sniffed. "Fis? (fish) In the outer room?" She was looking at a bundle of dried salmon we had hung in a corner. We had not noticed any odor, nor did we now, but Marian was showing us her sensibilities to any "stink."

The next time Thora came over she strode into the room, spread herself on the sea chest and announced imperiously she believed she'd have a cup of coffee. We could tell by the uncharacteristic shrill tone of her voice that she was excited. And she was—for a reason. She had just delivered the Charles baby—a fine big boy. Further, she had been given the privilege of thinking up a name and with what she felt to be a true stroke of genius had chosen "George," since it was close to George Washington's birthday. She left telling us she would have the boots finished for the "mans" outside right after conference.

While we waited for Mrs. Charles to recover enough that her husband Harold would be freed of household chores for our camping and movie making, we did what entertaining we could. We knew once we started camping there would be little chance to repay social obligations for after camping would come spring. And in spring came the most critical phase of our photography—the climax of the movie staged on the floating ice fields.

Still further impetus was given our entertaining with the arrival of a butchered and boned calf from friends in Matanuska Valley. Since the weather was fluctuating uncertainly above and below freezing we were afraid the meat might not keep, though we fashioned a refrigerator of corrugated paper and ice in the outer room. We thought it best to use as much as we could immediately.

One of the first we had over for supper was Dave.

As he had done all along, he went first to look over the puppies and particularly Sookgah. He ran his hand through Sooky's soft thick coat.

"He make nice parka ruff," he teased.

Then he opened Sooky's mouth and after inspecting the roof of it declared it "good." If it had been mottled he wouldn't have made a good sled dog, Dave declared.

"He's been running loose with the team," Fred told him.

"Good! Good! He young yet but he big enough."

Fred went on to tell him how Sooky had led the team all the way back on the last freighting trip and that we thought we could make a leader of him.

"How should we start training him to be a leader?" he asked.

Dave knew exactly. "You run him at swing (the position

behind the leader) for awhile. He won't like it because he'll want to lead, but he'll learn the pull of the harness and the lope that way. Then you run him next to Seegoo with a neck line attached to Seegoo. He a good looking dog," Dave finished. He thought the puppies were large enough to cut down to one feeding a day like the big dogs.

"That's good," Fred exclaimed, "less freight to take to camp."

"When you go to camp?" Dave wanted to know.

We told him just as soon as Mrs. Charles had regained her strength and Harold could leave.

"Well, hurry back," he said. "We miss you."

"We'll miss you, too."

"You think of me, it like my seeing you," he told us and somehow the phrase became a part of our memories.

We had the trader from St. Michael's in. He was on his way back after a winter "outside." Postmaster Ryan and his wife came for coffee and Swedish pancakes with lingonberries. We gave a birthday dinner for Howard. The evening Klopps spent with us, they brought the glad news we could order ice cream in bulk by the gallon air-freight from Anchorage. Several times that evening we heard sounds like rifle shots. It was our window panes cracking from a rapid drop in temperature and it continued on and off all night. We didn't expect to have a pane left when we arose in the morning but to our surprise they were all whole and again glazed with ice.

Another blizzard was raging.

We felt as if we were living in a tunnel with the windows completely buried. Fred went out four times to shovel so we could get some light, but before he was in the cabin the windows were plastered again. We wanted to get movies of the dogs in the blizzard but they wouldn't come out of their houses. Fred tried rattling the chains right outside each entrance—a sound which usually put them in a frenzy—but there was no visible reaction. We finally had to drag them out by their collars. Then Fred and Harold harnessed them and we took off for the flats for movie making under what proved to be the cruelest photographic conditions of our combined careers.

In monstrous stinging brush strokes, nature was slapping a paste of snow on everything. Immediately we merged into the white void—a ghostly caravan with every contrasting value obliterated except for the eyes of the dogs and our faces.

I looked at Fred. His nose was chalk white, his lashes weighted with beads of ice. "Your face is freezing," I yelled.

"Yours is too," he indicated my forehead.

We pulled off our fur mitts so we could get a hold on our handwarmers and our woolen undergloves were immediately coated with snow. The snow which wouldn't shake off melted when we put our mitts over them and then turned to ice. With bare hands we applied warmers to our frostbites, but by the time our faces would be thawed our hands would be starting to freeze. We tried to turn our backs to the savagery but the gusts were everywhere—crouched, ready to spring and, with teeth of ice, rake our flesh. If we had not taken handwarmers along that day we would no doubt have sustained severe frostbites.

There was a real hazard of getting lost.

I took Sookgah a short distance away so Fred could photograph him emerging out of the storm and when I turned Fred had been swallowed up in the nothingness. It was terrifying. I screamed—but my voice was only a finger tap against the roar of the wind. With no horizon, I could not tell whether I was stepping on snow or into air. I stumbled about sinking down to my hips in new snow, floundering helplessly, having to crawl or back up and start over and was completely done in when Sookgah led me back to Fred.

Even without the physical duress, the mechanical problems were enormous.

Fred worked bare-handed or with light cotton gloves, having ruined film before with hairs from his mitts and fuzz off the woolen gloves. We could only work minutes before the cameras started freezing. We would place them inside our parkas, but changing film was an impossibility. The snow was penetrable as air. The air was snow, an emulsion of snow. The effort ended when the main screw of our tripod snapped from the cold and the camera fell into a drift getting snow into the lens. We had to quit and felt we were extremely lucky to have exposed one hundred feet. We hoped for our pains we would have some dramatic storm shots, but no matter how dramatic, they could never compensate for the tortures of blizzard shooting.

Coming back into the village, there was no welcoming chorus from sled dogs. We could not see them and they, being deep in their houses or curled into balls, could not see us or hear us or smell us. The blizzard was a shroud smothering all the senses.

When we finally had the dogs unharnessed and dragged ourselves into the cabin, we collapsed on the bed for some minutes before we had strength to move. Our frostbites started aching and Fred pulled himself up to prod the fire. Then it was, that we noticed our mail on the table. There had been no plane that day. It must have arrived the day before and since we hadn't picked it up been brought in by Elizabeth or Alec. There were two packages. One was Floyd's Christmas present and the other was from my sister Francie in Tennessee. It was a bouquet of jonquil buds, still yellow, but never to blossom, for they too had been frozen and were just thawing out. Looking at them I was reminded that somewhere it was spring and—I could not hold back the tears.

CHAPTER

12

We were having winter's final fling, and a mighty fling it turned out to be.

There was one clear day so bright it was hard to tell whether the snow outdazzled the sun or the sky the snow. Fred and Harold took advantage of it to freight a load to the half-way mark and return that night. They reported rough going, with their former trail completely buried by deep drifts. Then the weather closed in again and supplies and camping equipment remained stacked in a corner of the cabin waiting for a second trip.

In between blizzards, a taste test of the snow revealed salt for the first time. We dug down under the top crust and found the snow pure again. There had been a west wind and we reasoned salt from the sea or sea ice had blown inland.

A plane came in with our first order of ice cream and together with the Russells and Klopps we put away the entire gallon at one sitting.

The missionary Londborg and his assistant, Spencer Strand, went for a two year's supply of wood, accompanied by certain of the villagers who would help on a share basis. All the trees had to be felled before break-up so their tractor could come back on the ice.

And in between blizzards, and during them too, we were beset by worry bitter as the winds because our shooting was falling farther and farther behind schedule. We were getting perilously close to spring—we realized it when the first birds flew up before us on our way to the Trading Post —and spring meant break-up, when the climax of our movie, the rescue from floating ice, must be photographed.

The condition of the ice field for our all-important sequence was extremely poor.

This year for the first and only time in the memories of the oldest residents of Unalakleet, the ice had frozen a record distance of fourteen miles out, and remained that way week after week, month after month. It had been so solid no storms had altered its surface.

There had been no breaking-up, no crashing together and grinding into pressure ice. For us, therefore, there was no photography of this spectacular far-northern phenomenon. Beside robbing us of choice, dramatic subject matter, the freak freeze-up had been a bane to the hunters of the village. For them, there were no leads where seal might surface for air and be hunted.

For neither photographers nor hunters was there any going to the edge of the field, since here the ice broke and reformed too thin to be safe.

We were all of us blocked by a great white desert as effectively as if it had been a sheer wall of ice. Worse yet, there was no improving the situation with a change of locale, since it was the same on the entire coast, or so our bush pilot friends, who were keeping an eye on it for us, reported. The only thing we could do (as we had done all winter long) was to watch for that first dark line in the white that meant open water. Only now as we watched, we hoped the ice wouldn't start breaking up, just as fervently as we had hoped all the previous months it would. Not until we could return from camping.

We had still other worries quite different from the weather, but also dealing with wondrous nature. Both Dave and Harold warned us that the female puppies might enter their breeding period any time and have to be isolated.

By mid-March we had to admit that our camping would now be "early spring" instead of "winter" as we had scheduled. It made no great difference as far as photographic conditions—there would still be snow and cold weather and the lighting would be much better—but for other reasons we were disappointed.

We had hoped to go on two camping trips, thus allowing ourselves a second chance should we encounter difficulties filming the first.

And secondly, we had counted on the spring camping trip to take the form of a vacation because long time friends, Ginny and Bill Belt, were coming from Ohio to go with us.

It was a trip the four of us had looked forward to from the time the movie project had been assured. Now, in spite of all our planning, photography would take up much of the time we had hoped to spend doing things with them.

Still, this turn of events wasn't as bad as it might have been for Ginny and Bill liked to be on their own. They had allowed us to hire their guide and team and order certain articles of clothing we considered necessary for their comfort. They had asked us to arrange a visit to an old-time fish trap and a flight to the edge of the ice to hunt seal, but other than these few accommodations they insisted upon being quite independent of us. Although we knew part of their insistence was out of respect for our movie project, we accepted it and appreciated it, since there was nothing else we could do.

Such a flexible arrangement was only possible between completely compatible companions.

At the same time, we did not worry about them for we knew they would follow excellent camping practises perfected on many high mountain pack-trips in the West.

All week, prior to the arrival of the Belts, the blizzards continued and then, magically, stopped, two days before we hitched up our team and mushed out to the air strip to meet them. We arrived just as they stepped off the plane —petite Ginny looking several sizes larger and Bill a blond giant, in their custom-made quilted suits. And if, when we saw them, we had a feeling of suddenly being in contact with a different world, we were certain they must have had the same feeling as they climbed into our sled.

From that moment began the fun of seeing the village as for the first time through their eyes. They could not believe the dogs would pull them through the deep snow and they marveled that Seegoo would go right or left by spoken word, without the use of reins.

The rest of that day we spent introducing them to our Native friends and it did not surprise us that they, like all newcomers, were struck by the friendliness and extreme politeness of all the villagers. Nor that they were impressed with the happy, red-cheeked children.

That night we gorged on shee fish—"the best fish I've ever tasted" Bill had declared—though we hardly found time to eat, there was so much to be said and sentences remained unfinished because there were so many subjects to be covered.

Unbelievably soon the time came for them to go to Postmaster Ryan's where they were quartered in a curtained-off corner of the room.

The next day we all left for camping.

With the wisdom of experience, Ginny and Bill had trained themselves into shape before they came. It was a good thing they had, for the trip turned out more rigorous than an auspiciously pleasant beginning indicated it might.

The morning was made for mushing, the air a heady stimulus that could not be denied. It stepped up the pace of the dog teams from a steady lope to a fancy prance and it caused us to leap from the sleds in sheer bursts of energy to call exuberantly to each other.

Harold lead the way with his five-dog team and a heavily loaded sled, followed by the Belts and their guide driving a seven-dog team. We brought up the rear with our big team and Sookgah, whom we had put in harness for the first time, to the side and a little behind Seegoo. To our surprise, Sookgah, instead of balking when harnessed, had happily busied himself pawing at Seegoo and mouthing great bites of fur. Seegoo, perhaps sensing the puppy's irresponsibility, bore it like a martyr but his revenge came shortly. When the signal was given to go, Seegoo had leaped forward with such vigor, the startled Sookgah had taken the first ten feet of the journey on his chin.

Harold followed a main route—the Unalakleet River. Already it was traveled enough to make a fast trail and the sleds skimmed along rocking slightly to the friendly squeak of the runners and soft thud of pounding paws. Sookgah skipped and pranced but soon began to realize it was easier to pace Seegoo and before a mile was done fell into the regular jog of the team.

Fred and Harold and the driver of the Belt's team rode the runners at the rear controlling the sleds with no more effort than an occasional slight shifting of weight.

We traveled in an excitingly pure world—gleaming, impeccable and soft of line, for all angles had been worn to roundness by the drubbing of the blizzard. Here and there, scallops and whorls and overhanging drifts, delicately modeled by an effulgent sun, gave design to the undulating white.

And then we came to the place we were to cut off for camp and found not the slightest trace of the trail Fred and Harold had broken. They walked back and forth searching minutely for any signs, they scanned the horizon, they felt about with their boots for any previously stamped down snow, but it was no use. The trail was gone and so— they ended up guessing the way.

Harold directed his dogs to turn and into the soft, deep snow they leaped up to their shoulders. Though they fought their way forward, Harold, after only a few minutes, stepped off the runners to help push.

Fred started pushing our sled, first chaining Sookgah to the rear. The puppy was gamely trying to keep up, but the snow was so deep he proved a drag on Seegoo, who was having a rough enough time as it was. I rolled off the sled and slipped into snowshoes to follow behind.

Soon Belt's team began to founder despite the fact Bill and then Ginny had alighted and taken to snowshoes for the first time in their lives. And so their driver began to push, too.

Our trip became a series of starts and stops with decreasing intervals of time between. Sometimes, the teams would bog down completely and when that happened, the drivers would slog to the front of the sled to give the towline a sharp, quick tug, pulling the team back enough so that they instinctively leaped forward.

But even this failed after a time and it became apparent the lead team was nearing exhaustion. Then it was that Harold, Fred, and Belt's driver, spelled off by Bill, did what all mushers are obliged to do at one time or another.

They took turns leading the way and by stamping down hard with snowshoes every step, broke a trail.

In this manner we proceeded for the better part of six hours when we finally came to the base camp Fred and Harold had established many weeks before. It had been an ordeal by snow; still, no one had complained or entertained any thought of turning back and so, eventually, we were able to joke about it.

Not, however, while we treadmilled the drifts to stake out our teams, or wrestled a cold, stiff tent with cold, stiff fingers or sawed and split wood or assembled the stove and stove pipe. But—when the lamp was lit, making our tent a glowing refuge in the forest gloom, when our socks and boots hung drying on the line by the ridge pole and when the little stove radiated heat from every surface, then, while we leaned back on our bed rolls and devoured plates of nourishing veal stew, the jokes came.

Directly after eating we crawled into our sleeping bags, but no sooner were we settled than the fearsome sound of a dog fight shattered the quiet. Fred bolted out, pulling on his trousers as he went. We had the running worry that Seegoo's face would be scarred or his ears chewed down and the ruckus was coming from the area where Seegoo was staked. Sure enough, Lynx had somehow slipped the bolt on his chain and made straight for Seegoo. To our utter astonishment, gentle Seegoo was standing Lynx off, or did, until Fred called to him sharply, whereupon our faithful pet folded his ears back, his eyes softened and he turned towards Fred, leaving himself completely defenseless against his attacker.

"I'll never stop him in a fight like that again before taking care of the other dog," Fred declared later. Still, the only blood drawn was a small gash on Lynx's foreleg.

Once peace was restored among our canine corps we

thought surely we would get some rest but our muscles, geared high for deep snow, seemed unable to return to neutral. No one objected when morning came and Fred reached out from the bag to stuff the little pile of shavings he had prepared the night before into the stove. And recovery began—with a steaming wash cloth to the face, and ointment for sun burns and adhesive patches for blisters and a breakfast of logger-sized pancakes, thick slab bacon and heroically strong coffee. After that, we were not only ready but eager to start up North River. Our dogs were ready, too, in spite of the punishment of the day before. They leaped into the air, howling joyfully, wrenching at their chains, Sookgah most enthusiastically of all.

Our trail was on the frozen river and, though a lovely smooth white pavement in appearance, Harold had to walk ahead on snowshoes probing with a pole every step of the way because, in reality, it was treacherous with open springs year-round. Sometimes a slight dip in the snow would give indication of these; sometimes, there was no sign at all.

At length we came to a high, spruce-dotted hill—a sugar loaf with raisins—which Fred had chosen to serve as a backdrop for shots of the dogs in action. A mile beyond this, on the high bank of a bend in the river, was the campsite he and Harold had scouted out weeks before.

It had everything we needed.

First of all, it was photogenic with well shaped spruce trees spaced just far enough apart to allow lovely patterns of sunlight and shade on the snow beneath. Second, the essentials of a good camp were there in abundance. We had a forest for firewood and we could get water from one of the springs in North River, instead of having to chop through the four to five feet of ice.

This time, when we made camp we did it with care since here would be our home for the entire month to come.

As we unharnessed the dogs and chained them out, we tamped the snow down for them. Then we fashioned nests of spruce bows so the snow where they lay would not turn to ice.

We set up our tent with good-sized spruce poles and banked the side walls with snow. Again we used spruce boughs for insulation between the tarpaulin which was the floor of the tent and the four feet of snow it sat on. The stove we placed just inside the left flap and our supplies on the right, and the rear we allotted to sleeping bags. Lastly, we placed a "beating stick" beside the entrance. This was to knock snow off our boots before coming inside where it might melt and wet them. The thud of wood on skin took the place of a door knocker.

Once the camp was set up, Fred and Bill started chain sawing to make the wood supply "strong" and Harold went to locate a spring for water. He decided to try first where there was a dip in the snow-covered frozen river close to shore. Carrying a long pole and tapping warily as a blind man he approached until, all at once, the pole plunged, meeting no resistance and came up dripping. It was the most successful "well witching" we had ever seen. All he did was brush the snow aside so we would know where to step, dipped a bucket in, and set it down outside our tent. Ice crystals started forming in it immediately and when Bill went to get a dipper full of water a few moment later, he had to break a thin skim of ice.

That night, though no one went out to look at the thermometer, we knew there was a decided drop in temperature because the opening of our sleeping bag wore a collar of hoar frost when we awakened in the morning. We had used both our inner and outer bags and since one of them was supposed to be adequate to zero and the two together comfortable to 40 below, we guessed the temperature to have been around minus thirty. The Belts did not have as elaborate bags as we did, but they managed to keep warm by adding mitts and extra socks, scarves and chest protectors to their quilted suits. It was a great joke we batted back and forth over our tarpaulin partition—how they dressed to go to bed while we, in true trail fashion, stripped to our nethermost. They had the edge of getting up, however, until we perfected a system of pulling our clothes inside our sleeping bag in the morning for a predressing warm-up.

After that first night it got warm enough for us to use just the outer bag to sleep in with the second one over us. Days, the temperature would range to the twenties though usually not above zero before noon. Still, any food more than four feet from the stove would remain frozen. It didn't matter since we used dried staples except for bread, meat and leftovers and for these, thawing became as much a part of preparing meals as cooking. We were careful not to touch aluminum utensils when our hands were damp as they would stick and might pull away the flesh.

The temperature did not hamper our picture-taking as much as we had feared. We found we could make efficient use of our time by working around camp or exploring possible locations in the morning and doing our photography in the afternoon. With the sun working longer hours each day, there was a welcome increase in shooting time. Beginning after lunch, we would expose as much film before our evening meal as we had worked three days to expose in midwinter.

And then it warmed up enough so that we could shoot morning and afternoon and that was what we did, day after lengthening day, stopping only to wave Ginny and Bill off on one of their side trips, and then to welcome them back as if they had been around the world twice. And, finally, after two weeks, we went back with them to Unalakleet, they to catch their plane, we to stand and gaze. Our thoughts were air-borne with them and for those moments we felt dislocated—completely, depressingly displaced.

They were returning to familiar things, known and dear, things we had left a year ago and which we would not see for another half year. We would miss Ginny and Bill. With true sophistication, they had adapted themselves perfectly. The hours on trail and the evenings in camp we would have enjoyed ourselves, we had enjoyed even more with them.

As we talked over their visit on our way to the village, we had a premonition that the Belts might be but the first of many to spend a vacation on trail in the far north, that in the future, Unalakleet might become a mecca for tourists. Only, most tourists would not be like the Belts and Unalakleet, when that time came, would never be the Unalakleet we had known.

Having allowed these "off project" thoughts on top of a vacation—notably discontinuous, but a vacation,—we now took ourselves sternly in hand and went looking for Howard to return to camp for more photography.

CHAPTER

13

Howard was waiting for us at the cabin and he was the most excited little Eskimo we'd ever seen. We didn't know whether it was his being excused from school or the prospects of camping or the new shotgun we had surprised him with, but whether one or all three, the sun shone extra brightly for him that afternoon.

One small shadow crossed it, however.

Since we would be photographing Howard and Harold on the trip out, and since we had not worked the shiny new shotgun into our script, we had to ask that it be placed beneath the sled cover. Howard quickly agreed (though his hands refused to move as quickly in the putting away of the new treasure). But Harold—Harold simply could not understand at all. Once we convinced him that we meant it, he just stood, shaking his head and pressing his lips together hard to keep from saying what he thought. To Harold, being on the ready for game was as much a part of the trail as the sled or the dogs.

Being without the shotgun didn't bother Howard at all once we were started. Regally he lolled atop the load, supreme sovereign of the sled train. When we had him drive for our cameras he was a little nervous, though glad afterward that he'd had the nerve to do it.

As soon as we pulled into camp, Harold and Fred started unharnessing the dogs and unloading the sleds, while I gathered spruce boughs to place beneath the runners so they wouldn't sink in or freeze to the snow.

For these camping activities, Howard had no interest. While we carried them on, he scrambled to the top of the highest spruce tree to get some "spruce gum" to chew.

"Boy, oh boy, that's good," he declared, gnawing at the outside only, since the inside had the flavor of turpentine.

In the mornings, before the sun had warmed to a point of photography, Howard was free to go as he pleased. This might mean hunting with his new shotgun or setting a trap for a "camp robber" (jay) which had been pecking away at our sacks of dog food or just exploring on snow shoes. In the beginning we were afraid he might get lost but he always came back so far ahead of time for lunch that we soon stopped worrying.

Every step off beaten trails now had to be taken on snow-shoes or else we would sink over our boot tops and some-times to our hips. This made our photography physically taxing for though we had snowshoes, Howard had none, Harold had loaned his out and so we had to give them ours when we photographed them. We soon learned the way to get snow out of one's boots was to lie on one's back on the ground and shake it out.

One morning after our dogs had sounded several alarms during the night, Harold came hurrying to our tent to report fresh tracks in the snow. We followed him to a spot not fifty yards from camp and though he had to tell *us*, two paw marks side by side with a crescent marking off each two pairs, told *him*, a wolverine had called. Harold was even more excited about tracks farther down the river—not the many kidney shaped prints marking where a rabbit had paused or the pacer trail of the fox, but the bovine-like track of a moose, which were just beginning to be seen for the first time in this area of Alaska.

Harold knelt down and felt the tracks.

"They're fresh," he told us positively.

"How do you know?"

"No crust on them." He pointed to nearby fresh droppings to corroborate his statement. "I think I'll go after him."

And there went our movie-making for that afternoon. Yet we knew from experience nothing would be gained by asking Harold to stay in camp. Even though we were paying him for it, he would have been disgruntled. And that would have been out of character for the Eskimo in our script! So instead, we told Howard to take the afternoon off too, to hunt rabbits. Howard was back long before supper, Harold not until an hour afterward. No moose was shot nor any rabbits, but they were both happier for having had the chance to do some of the things they felt should be done when camping.

At the end of our fourth week out, the snow started getting so soft we would occasionally break through while wearing snowshoes. By that time we had covered the subject matter called for in our camping sequence; still, we stayed on unable to resist the perfect photographic weather.

Then Harold, who was supposed to have taken a day off for hunting, returned within an hour to state flatly that the time had come to leave because the river was getting dangerous.

We wasted no time following his suggestion. We had not the slightest intention of being stranded upriver by break-up. Not with so much shooting to be done back at the village. Not with the puppies to be broken to harness before the filming of the climax on floating ice.

While we broke camp and packed, Harold equipped each sled with a "gee" pole. These were small trees, cut six feet in length and stripped. They were then lashed to one side of the sled projecting two to three feet beyond the basket. They would be particularly useful in keeping the sleds on trail which was now a hard packed "spine" with deep mushy snow on either side.

In record time we were ready and on our way with only a backward glance—only one—but that was enough for the emptiness to reproach us. The black hole the stubborn little stove had melted in a gradual descent to bare ground, the spruce-bough nests of the dogs, the trails now silent and untouched, the scars and by-products of living—gashes on the trees from the dog chains, wood chips, the "beating stick" lying forlornly on the ground—all called to us that here once was warmth and nourishment and peace of heart and here again it could be. We looked away quickly but it was too late. A little part of our hearts had chosen to remain on the high bank of a bend of North River.

I drove the dogs while Fred rode the bumper so when the sled side-slipped into deep snow, he could jump off and guide it back again with the "gee" pole.

Sookgah still ran beside Seegoo but now, without any foolery, he fell immediately into the steady lope of the team. When we came to an old cutoff he had taken on his first trip to camp and he tried to veer away on it we were pleased mightily, for that meant Sookgah had a good nose for picking out trails, an important requisite for a leader.

On our way we noticed large patches of brown tundra showing on the south side of slopes or where the snow had lain thin. In the village itself there was bare ground between the shrunken snow banks and on one of these was scraped a hopscotch pattern—a sure sign of spring.

An even more momentous change was the completely exposed main path. It had been cleared by a bulldozer from the army site for the Spring Conference, which had taken place while we were away.

The same day we returned we ran into Dave whose proud job it had been to interpret announcements and sermons at the mission conference. As we walked with him over a side path still intersected with snow banks, but in which steps had been carefully cut for the conference, he talked about it.

The men had brought in supplies of wood and ice beforehand so there would be no time lost from visiting. In this, they had shown foresight because there had been many visitors—153 with thirty-seven teams of 231 dogs in all. The influx had been a drain on village supplies but with donations and the extra bread the women had baked ahead of time, there had been enough.

All of the services had been held in the new mission with one of them taking the form of a formal dedication. There had been meetings—two and sometimes three a day.

"That mission bell ring so much, it like an air raid," Dave grinned. But not quite. The air-raid alarm for the village was the simultaneous ringing of the school bell and both the old and new mission bells. "How the puppies?"

"Fine," Fred told him. "We're going to try them in harness this week."

"You run dem all togedder?" Dave was incredulous.

Fred nodded. "We haven't time to break them in with the big team."

"Boy! That will be someting to see!"

And "someting to see" it was—a "someting" that was a pandemonium of sound and confusion.

At the sight of the harnesses, the big team had, as they always did, begun to howl and bay and jump up on top of their houses and down again. The puppies, except for Sookgah, didn't understand the reason for the ruckus but not wishing to miss out on anything, added their chorus.

First, we harnessed Seegoo and beside him Sookgah. Sooky, who should have known better by this time, succumbed to the mass hysteria and began chewing at Seegoo and turning back to bark as the puppies were hitched behind him. We put Kinguk at swing and while he snapped at Sooky's tail and pawed at him, brought up Newcah. This precipitated a tussle ending with Kinguk's leg tangled in his neck strap and Newcah half out of harness. I knelt to straighten her out and as I did she leaped up hitting my right eye so hard, the tears streamed. Meanwhile, Fred and Harold brought over the next two, Mik-nik-rok and Kahfik. For a moment it seemed we might be making progress but when we looked around we found Sooky had chewed through his harness. While this was being tied together, See-oo-ti and Nanny were harnessed. Being at the wheel next to the sled and farthest from the others only made them more frantic to join the melee. They squirmed and bit at the straps and wrestled each other and yapped constantly to more than fill any breathing spells of their fellow brawlers.

We would think they were all set and give the signal to Seegoo and Sooky only to find one or several caught in their harnesses and have to stop again. On one of these stops, Nanny chewed through her tug line.

At last, we reached the Bering Sea ice field, some half out of their harnesses, some tangled and running on three legs and one turned around backwards but once we were able to get them all straightened out and started off with a smooth trail underfoot, they worked incredibly well.

"They work like they were born in harness," Harold

said, and it was true. There was no balking and no rolling. Heeling out against the pull of their lines, backs arched, paws digging deeply, they impelled themselves forward. Their power amazed us. Either Fred or Harold or I would ride the brake and still they pulled so hard the snow would spray in our wake and the sled hurtle at top speed.

We let them gallop, hoping they would start to tire but this had no effect whatsoever. Except on poor Seegoo who was completely bewildered at not being able to settle down into his regular energy-saving lope for fear of being over-run. Once we stopped them to brush snow off their chins and inspect their paws for ice and when we did, they promptly and thoroughly tangled their trappings. There-after, when we stopped for movie taking or any other rea-son, we unfastened their tuglines, leaving them harnessed only by the shorter necklines.

We ran them for over an hour and they never showed the slightest sign of fatigue. The only one to slow down at all was Kinguk and that was to balk at open water. When we left the ice field they put on an extra burst of speed be-cause they knew they were headed for the cabin and food.

From then on we stepped up the puppy training, running them at least once, sometimes twice a day. We wanted to make certain they would be completely broken to harness by the time the Bering Sea field broke and we had to take them out on the floating ice to photograph our climax. Everywhere were reminders that this time was not far off.

It was in the frost crystals which glittered in the air. It was in the pools of surface water forming on the ice field. We felt the urgency even more when Lynx's tail as-sumed a proud new angle as he regarded Nanny chained nearby.

The time came when we thought Sookgah was ready to

Howard and the shotgun he earned.

Tracks in the snow tell a story to Harold.

Our cabin after each blizzard.

Lunch on the trail: frozen sandwiches and thermoses of hot tea.

Marian "Miowak" Gonongnan and her husband, Miles, with the author.

Mahsengah and her family.

Easter time was a time to "dress up".

Women and girls gather willow shoots.

Howard is "hooking" or fishing for tomcod.

The author helps Mother Geenah feed the puppies.

Fred filming the climax of our movie.

lead alone and so we left Seegoo behind. Sookgah did not, as we had hoped, sprint unswervingly forward. Instead he bounced along, first to the right and then to the left and tiring of this, turned to spar with Kinguk. It was necessary for Fred again to take over the role of lead dog—to run ahead while I held the puppies, the brake locked in a crack or in hard snow until he called them. As long as Fred was ahead, Sookgah could hardly be held back and when given the signal to go would lead the team at a top gallop while I rode the brake with both feet and used all my strength to control the careening sled. It was on these sprints that Sookgah must have acquired the feel of pulling for we began to notice that on the return trip to the cabin he was keeping the towline straight. Then, gradually, out on the ice field, he began to pay less and less attention to Kinguk and to take the business of leading more seriously. By the time Fred was jogging along beside him with a neckline to train him on "gee" and "haw," Sookgah felt he had to run at least half a length ahead. It was then we knew we had a leader and not only that, but an extremely good-looking one. The entire team was spectacularly photogenic with Sookgah individually marked, and the six puppies behind him paired off as identical twins. One feature of his make-up remained a mystery as yet and that was whether or not Sookgah's ears would be erect. Though the five sisters' ears were entering various stages of ascending, the ears of the two males, Sooky and Kinguk, remained bouncing triangles. This did not worry us. It was perfectly legitimate for them to have floppy ears since the Malemute breed had either type. As it was, the uncertain angle of Sooky's ears gave him an upstart appearance that contrasted wonderfully with his father's natural majesty.

Often we took Howard on the puppy runs so he would become used to handling them, and to get movies of this phase of their training. Such a magnificent picture they all made —the puppies in the prime of condition, galloping open-mouthed, as if laughing, and their young Eskimo master grinning with excitement—that we were tempted to put aside our cameras to just look and enjoy.

It was upon our return to the village from one of these runs that we heard the news. Dave had died of a heart attack.

The fact was hard to accept. Lovable, mischievous, generous-hearted, intelligent Dave. No more hunting of whales for him, no more posing as he had often done for Fred in the past, no more lessons in the Eskimo language for me or suppers together with old-time stories. Dave wouldn't even see our puppies run as a team.

We remembered something Dave had said. "You think of me, it like my seeing you."

You have seen us many times, dear friend. . . .

CHAPTER

14

"Luke! (look) Machetanz, luke!"

Great-grandmother Marian belly flopped to the ground, arched her back like a gondola and coasted down the two story high snow bank.

As she skidded to a halt, she jumped up, snatched the line of the little sled she had sent scudding ahead and, half-dancing, pulled it over the sand and dirt and up the next drift. This time at the top she placed one knee on the sled and using her other leg as a pusher made another quick descent. Near the bottom, the sled slowed in soft snow but only momentarily for with another push, Marian sent it on to the frozen river mouth and there it gained enough momentum to glide in among the varicolored parkas of tomcod fishers before coming to a stop.

Marian bounced off and turning back yelled, "Where I fis, Machetanz?"

Marian asked because she herself had not had a tomcod hole that winter and it was against all etiquette to fish anybody else's. To take movies of her fishing, we had engaged someone to chip and dig out a hole and quite a job it had been with the ice over four feet thick.

We found the proper hole, Marian pulled the sled up, took off the foot and a half pole tied to it and sat down. I leaned over to look.

"No! no!" she pushed me back grinning. "Don't luke in hole in spring. Scare fis away." Almost at the same moment she clapped her hand to her mouth. "I *mean* unless your face blacked," she added hurriedly and burst into whoops of laughter at her slip of the tongue.

Marian was having a wonderful time. It was a gorgeous day to be out with the ten-above weather much warmer in the sun—so warm, the snow was steaming. She liked to have her picture taken and here she was being paid for something she liked to do. To top it off, fishing was good. Bringing up a tomcod was almost a reflex to lowering the red beaded unbarbed hook into the water. In a short time, Marian had filled the sack she had brought along and we had filled out cameras with exposed film. Still, she was enjoying herself so much she decided to stay on and visit with some of her cronies and so we started back through the village alone.

Up and over snow banks shrunk to half their size. They were going so fast the villagers were filling every available vessel—barrels, washtubs, drums—anything, against the time when there would be no snow to melt for washing. Drinking water still came from upriver but the getting of it was now dangerous. Already the ice had separated from the bank in several places and one had to be careful to avoid dark water on the ice for that was where the river was coming through.

Through the square we walked, now completely bare and dried enough for games of marbles. Children shouted happily with games of tag and rolled hoops. Among them we spotted Number six choreboy who had quit because "too much work at home in spring" and had been replaced by Number seven.

Everywhere was the bustle and activity of villagers gathering refuse of winter in piles to burn, raking over last year's gardens.

"I see sea gull!" a boy called excitedly from a roof top.

"What does that mean?" Fred asked.

"Warm weather!" he told us.

Perhaps he had been watching for his father or his brother out seal hunting. Though the ice still remained frozen from fourteen to eighteen miles out, the villagers felt compelled to hunt because it was the time of year for it. Very few seals were brought in for usually the hunters would find the field unsafe at the edge. But once in a while one would be lucky enough to be there when the newly formed ice had broken off and gone out to sea and there was strong, thick ice next to the water.

From hoping desperately that the ice field would break up and go out when we had first returned from camp, we were now hoping just as fervently that it would hold. One of the females—Nanny—had entered her breeding period and was being cloistered in a rented dog barn.

Our cabin, along with all the houses, emerged whole as the snow drifts melted away from them. Now as we approached, late in the afternoon, no light showed from the window. There was not the need, with the sun beginning to shine at four in the morning and not setting until sixteen hours later. As we came up to the cabin we stopped talking and listened.

Sarah and Ruthie had evolved a new game—that of hide-and-seek. Whenever they saw us approaching, they would take cover to remain hidden until we had hunted them out. We looked behind the outer door and between the stove and washstand and behind the table and found them—one behind the inner door and the other standing atop the toilet in the outer room. When they pulled themselves together from giggling, Sarah came forth with the usual.

"I've got news!"

"What?"

"It's spring!"

"How do you know?"

She paused, considering and then, "The weather tell me so."

"It tell me too," I answered, taking off my rubber boots and slipping into leather moccasins. They felt wonderfully light after a winter in fur boots and two pairs of thick socks but at the same time a little more snug than when I had worn them last.

Fred went out to chisel ice from around the window so it could be opened. As I watched him, it set me to remembering—remembering that just a year ago I had looked out that window on a sight I would never forget.

It had been a procession—a small, sad, straggly procession. First there had been the air-lines truck, not top-heavy with its usual load of freight and children clinging to its sides but with a single cargo—a coffin of green boards. Behind that was a tractor pulling a sledge and on it women doubled in grief and behind them, men walking with the blanched faces of those who have to do with death.

Another pilot had been killed—the brother of the bush pilot serving Unalakleet. Another air-borne knight of the back country—patrolman of the skies and the trails and the ice, purveyor of supplies and passengers, message bearer, errand boy, archangel of mercy. Another winged pioneer who had blazed his trails with skid marks on sand bars and in the parallel grooves of skis on frozen lakes and who, having once opened the country, became the link between what was and what was to be—wings clipped, forever.

He was not the first in the family for there had been flying brothers. Nor was he the only bush pilot that year. To other families of bush pilots had come the numbing disbelief, the smothering anxiety, the bargains with God, the SEARCH.

The SEARCH:

Upon that everything depended—the tenure of a family; the release of completion for the searchers or the denial of it by a shadow, a canyon, a patch of trees; and, for the hunted—life itself.

The SEARCH:

For crippled aircraft or broken bodies—to each plane an area thirty miles in length to be scanned mile-wide by mile-wide strip, then to zig-zag across it diagonally like the mending of a tear. It was best to have an observer with each pilot, the one to tend to flying, the other to look. If this prescribed procedure was followed, the SEARCH should be sixty to ninety percent effective. If the pilot belonged to the Civil Air Patrol, the army furnished gasoline. If not, the pilot would assume the cost or—the pilot's widow.

The SEARCH:

An impersonal, mathematical formula that denied the agonies, the heroisms, the oneness behind it.

Unalakleet was caught up in the SEARCH. There was talk of nothing else. All thinking was of it, all hoping, all hopelessness, all grieving. When it was done with, villagers again went their way, thinking their own thoughts, but the village was stronger for having hoped the same hope and for having sorrowed together when that hope had not come true.

The window was open.

Once more the smells and the sound of a whirring wind-charger established communication with the outdoors.

And sounds in the night, too. Of the dogs in a frenzied chorus when early-rising seal hunters took off. Of a post being dragged over the snow reminding us we must have Number seven choreboy help dig post holes in the ground now that the ice in which they were set was thawing. When a puppy did pull free, it was not such an ordeal to chase out after it or to send stray dogs on their way. And when we crawled back in bed, it was between sheets of linen instead of flannel.

There were sounds of mice tunneling between our log walls and the sod banking and one morning, an hour before sunrise, of the single note of a guitar followed by a low melodious chorus of an Easter hymn.

Easter was another important event in church life, with live Easter lilies being flown in from Anchorage for the altar. Again the children "spoke pieces." We took pictures for Reverend Londborg—it was easy to find shots that were colorful and appealing, with all the little girls in summery dresses and hair ribbons and one matron with her four little daughters dressed in matching parkas.

Once Easter was over, the village turned its thoughts to the farewell party to be held for Nurse Jette who was being transferred, since her office was due to change over from the Native Service to Alaska Public Health.

It was to be a surprise and so the Russells had detained Miss Jette at dinner beforehand while the guests had slipped into the basement of the school. Every adult in the village had been invited and it appeared all invitations were accepted.

There was an opening prayer and then several songs by the Mothers' Club and the Male Chorus. The Mothers'

Club, National Guard, Sewing Circle, Mission Helpers, PTA, Midwives, Alaska Crippled Children's Association—all had farewell gifts for Miss Jette, presented with tears of appreciation and a speech by a selected representative. Miss Jette, in turn, gave up swabbing her glasses and removed them entirely to let the tears course down her cheeks unchecked.

One gift particularly cherished was the "friendship apron" with signatures of all her friends embroidered on it, and there was a guest book for which Fred had done the cover.

Then came refreshments and what a repast it was with an entire case of cake mix having been baked, dishpans full of jello, and ham sandwiches flown in from Anchorage by order of the trader.

With Miss Jette's going, there was no medical assistance in the village other than advice given by short wave over the radio to the Russells, and it was just at this time that Fred noticed a bulge in his right groin. Not having the time to spare from photography for a flight to Anchorage, he did what any artist would do—made a sketch of his pelvic section and sent it to our doctor. The diagnosis came by return air mail. "You have made a perfect sketch of an inguinal hernia." Following the precautions he advised, Fred finished out the year normally and we were perfectly satisfied with our diagnosis by post. So was our doctor who had also written, "I am keeping your sketch as a self portrait of Machetanz."

Coincident with Miss Jette's departure, there were other departures from the village for spring was a time of exodus.

Lillian noticed a falling off in school attendance as children went out with their families to camp. So went our Number seven choreboy, replaced by Number eight. Some went to trap squirrels, others to gather greens. The first "greens" of the year were a kind of miniature cotton plant growing out of the hummocks on the tundra. The half inch white root was considered quite a delicacy. Next came low shoots which would be mixed with small serrated leaves growing directly off the ground and put up in seal oil for next winter's salad. Other greens grew on the beach and resembled sauerkraut in flavor. These were boiled and put away to be eaten the following spring.

Elizabeth left off plucking goosedown for a quilt to go gather alder bark. This she would cut into shavings, which combined with lye made an effective reddish brown dye for seal skin. Dyeing enhanced the value of the skins but Elizabeth had few to work with this year due to the condition of the ice.

Hunters continued to go out, if not after seal, for bears or after the wild fowl beginning to take over the skies.

Spring was in full swing and still the entire coast of Norton Sound was reported icebound by the bush pilots. They had now changed from skis to wheels, the ice of the rivers being too rotten to be safe.

We continued to run the puppies daily but we put the trail-wise Seegoo back ahead of Sookgah because the ice was getting dangerous—honeycombed with holes and covered with sheets of surface water. It began to look as if the field would simply disintegrate and never break up.

With the completion of our movie held up until the icefield broke, we were gripped by restlessness. When we could stand the waiting no longer, we decided to take a trip to get more movies of Harold mushing on the icefield and at the same time film the reindeer which had come down to the coast for fawning. We felt doing something—going somewhere—even though it wasn't getting our sled dog movie finished—would be a relief.

The plan was for us to drive the puppies led by Seegoo and Sookgah and Harold would use our adult team with his leader.

On the day set for departure, we packed our sleds and harnessed both teams and then we sat and waited for Harold. Minutes went by and finally an hour. We should have suspected something had gone wrong since he was never late but we didn't and so were not prepared for a set-back. When he arrived, it wasn't to go with us but to tell us he "had an emergency"—an infected gland—and would be leaving for the hospital the next day.

We were stimply staggered. First, of course, was real concern for Harold's health and secondly, we felt our entire project wrecked. Besides Howard, Harold had the most important role in our movie. We had worked with him all winter and shot the activities in season that it would be impossible to repeat. Around him revolved the final rescue sequence.

"When will you be back?" Fred asked trying to sound matter of fact.

"Don't know," Harold replied. "Better not count on me."

We both felt sick with disappointment but no matter how we felt, there was nothing to be done but to wish him well. We watched him walk back towards his home and years of plans and hopes and months of punishing work were trampled with every step he took. I burst into tears and turned to Fred.

He was tapping a tooth, thinking. "You know, we might run in a substitute. If we could get somebody about the same size . . ."

"We could borrow Harold's clothes—" I followed up quickly. Anything rather than throw the whole project over.

"And it's spring. He would be wearing dark glasses out on the ice."

The more we talked the more it seemed possible to carry on with a substitute. We began naming over men who might be suitable and after discussing and eliminating them for one reason or another ended up with one man—Pete Katongan. True, Pete had more gray hair than Harold but this, we decided, wouldn't matter if he kept his parka hood up.

Leaving the teams still harnessed, Fred hurried over to see Pete only to be handed another disappointment. Pete had gone seal hunting and would not be back for several days. That eliminated taking movies of a stand-in for Harold on our trip but since we were all ready and there seemed no reason to do otherwise, we decided to go. We asked Alec, just for the pleasure of his company and he, in turn, was so pleased he came with his gear within the hour.

And so we started out—Alec in the lead with Harold's leader and our big dog team and us following with Seegoo and Sookgah leading the puppy team. It wasn't a good day for photography anyway, we told ourselves, with the sun filtering through a cloud layer and making a diffused light. There were no shadows and everything appeared in one tone of gray. Still, the light was so bright that my eyes hurt without dark glasses.

Instead of heading out towards the sea as Harold had planned to do, we chose to short-cut along the coast but very soon we realized we had made a bad decision. Inshore, there were masses of pressure ice left from the fall storms and all still covered with deep snow so that we could not tell where there was any solid footing and where there were snow-bridged chasms. We crashed over and thudded against tent sized boulders of ice. I scrambled along beside Seegoo while Fred heaved the sled around. Suddenly I stepped into a deep concealed crack and sunk to my waist,

Seegoo on top of me. The sudden pull threw the sled into a crevasse leaving puppies clawing desperately at sheer ice or dangling helplessly in the air. While I tried to boost Seegoo up and off me, Fred made prodigious efforts at getting the sled righted. Alec secured the big team and came back to help us for the puppy harnesses were in a hopeless snarl. So our sledding went, for over half of that fourteen-mile trip, yet the puppies went like a racing team—up to their chins in snow and water, treadmilling the cracks, they never once lowered their tails or seemed anything less than possessed to go forward.

In midafternoon we came again to smooth ice and stopped for lunch. We took out our canned meat and hardtack and tea and turning over our sled as a brake to hold the team, sat on it. Alec preferred to stand and scan the horizon for seals. Twice cranes flew over and another time a large flock of geese. Alec called them with an exact imitation of their honk but they were too far away to heed.

Then came still another trying episode.

Lynx jumped his teammate Arbo. There were no preliminary arched backs or stiff-legged walking or warning snaps. Instead there was all at once a horrendous growling and death-dealing lunges with bared fangs. The rest of the team turned, hesitating for just a moment and in that moment, Fred was able to grab the leader. I saw Seegoo start up and over followed by the puppy team anxious to join the fracas. It might well have been the end of our movie, had the dogs tangled their harnesses, but Seegoo still retained enough civilizing discipline to be stayed by a shouted "no," until I could lead him away by the collar. Bright red splotches began to show in the snow as Alec ran to grab a chain from the back of the sled. When he rushed back to the dogs and raised his arm I looked away. Again and again I heard the chain hit flesh before the fighting stopped. There were no yelps of pain, only, after endless minutes, a cessation of growling. Once the dogs were pulled apart we were dumfounded to find Arbo without a scratch. Lynx, the trouble maker, was again the victim of his love of fighting. His ear was ripped and blood was spurting from a foreleg. Alec knelt to staunch the flow with snow and again Fred and I were thinking "here could go our movie." If Lynx could not run again, there would be no more pictures of the big team for Lynx was so uniquely marked and colored, there was no replacement for him in the village.

With the bleeding stopped, we chained Lynx apart from the team and Alec went back to his lunch.

"You can't eat?" he asked me.

I shook my head.

"I'm sorry I had to use the chain."

"I know. There was no other way . . ."

When we started out, Alec left Lynx's tugline loose so that he had no weight to pull. Still he tired quickly and the bleeding started again so Alec lifted him into the sled.

It wasn't until late afternoon we began to see the half-dozen deserted cabins and trading post of what had been the village of Egavik. They sat in a row with openings that once were windows staring vacantly out to sea. Behind them stretched the broad valley of the Egavik River already running brown water at its mouth and too treacherous for the dogs. Again we fought our way through a jungle of inshore ice before we came scraping up on the rocky shore.

Alec, who had already staked his dogs out, came to help with ours.

"Elmer is here," he told us. "He wants us to come for coffee."

To us—exhausted, soaked, bruised and discouraged, nothing could have sounded better. In addition, Elmer was the herder of the reindeer and he could tell us where they were and what chance we stood of getting pictures of them.

CHAPTER

15

While we drank strong black coffee and ate chunks of bread torn off a loaf fresh baked by Mrs. Elmer Kotongan, her husband talked of the reindeer.

To our first question "Where are they?" he gave a welcome answer "Just over the hill about a mile and a half."

He told us the bucks had separated from the does during fawning season and that he had been having trouble keeping them together as a herd. He told us, too, that there was a lone wolf around which had killed four of the fawns and that he had taken a shot at it and missed.

We asked where we should pitch our tent.

"You can use cabin," he told us and after we had finished our coffee showed us which one. It was difficult to visualize our decrepit little shack as once having been part of a meat packing center complete with a slaughterhouse and storage facilities. That had been when the reindeer herds were privately owned and numbered in the thousands rather than the hundreds. With the herds sold to the Government, who sponsored them as an industry for the natives, the management of Egavik had left and soon the rest of the villagers followed for the reason most isolated natives came to villages—so their children could go to school.

Since then, the cabins had been used very occasionally by the herder's families and by people traveling like ourselves. Ours, though filled with litter, had not been vandalized in any way. The only pieces of equipment we unpacked from our sled were our little thin metal stove and pans, since our cabin was already furnished with a built-in bunk bed, two tables, chairs and a stool.

On shelves over the tables, I transferred the contents of our food boxes packed to prepare meals on short notice. One box, the breakfast box, contained pancake mix, syrup, coffee, shortening, powdered egg, milk and sugar. In a second box for the evening meal were dried fruits, canned meat, hardtack, dehydrated potatoes and onions and in a third box miscellaneous kitchen supplies such as paper towels, soap and flour. We had learned if we packed the same for every trip, we always knew where to find things.

Once our dishes were on the table, a stack of driftwood by the stove and a bucket of water by the wash basin, we felt "at home" and we knew still another small piece of our hearts would stay here on a high rocky bank to watch the vast sweep of the Bering Sea.

Before turning in, we checked Lynx. We had made a soft bed of grass for him and taken out extra food and water during the evening. His leg wound appeared to be closing nicely.

The next morning we set out early and on foot to hunt the herds a "mile and a half away."

First was the crossing of the river. We found the surface ice overrun with brackish water from wide, deep cracks and it was not without going in over the ankles of our shoepacks that we were able to get across. On the other side, a steep bluff awaited us. So steep it was, we had to crawl to keep from being pulled backwards by our heavily loaded packs.

Once on top, we had smooth walking for a time over flat rocks but when we started down we came to singularly difficult terrain. Hummocks of grass from which the soil had fallen away gave an impression of a plain of huge hassocks. Sometimes they were close together, allowing us to jump from one to the other but elsewhere they were wider apart, compelling us to weave around and between. When we did that, we sloshed in water from the thawing ground, prime breeding grounds for mosquitoes.

There were draws to be crossed where the snow lay hip-deep but with the crust so soft we broke through and there were entangling clumps of alders.

Only occasional patches of thin snow showed on the brown hills—sugar frosting soaked into dark gingerbread were what they looked like. It was the exact color combination of the reindeer and fawns, which we didn't catch a glimpse of until after six hours of walking.

First we had seen their antlers over the crest of a hill and so we had crept up quietly to find seven deer and their fawns.

Stealthy though our approach, they somehow sensed us and took flight, one female deserting her fawn. Elmer had told us the does would sometimes never come back so rather than cause the fawn's starvation, we retreated without taking a picture and watched out of camera range until the mother returned and led it off.

Then, on again, down to the hummocks, over the draws, up the endless hills dotted with spruce trees stripped when the deer had rubbed velvet from their horns the summer before. In late afternoon, Alec, who had reconnoitered far and wide, came back to tell us he had spotted deer. The herd was made up of females and their fawns and was only over the next two hills, but by then it was too late for movie taking.

Wearily we started back, sinking to our knees in the fragrant tundra many times before reaching the cabin. It had been another frustrating day added to the several frustrating developments of the spring. If ever we were discouraged and felt we'd had our fill of photography, it was then.

Yet, some twenty-four hours later when we followed the same route back to our cabin, it was with an enormous enthusiasm for our work—the only difference being the film in our packs had been exposed.

We had found the reindeer that next day only an hour and a half's hike away.

First, we had heard the irregular ringing of bells, muted and far away. Then, we had come upon the bulls, easily detectable since they had already shed their antlers, and farther on—cows and wobbly legged fawns. They were all colors, from chocolate brown to the near orange of a chipmunk. There were no all white ones but many were spotted with white while some appeared to be wearing black socks.

They were feeding around a frozen lake on the tender shoots coming out of the tundra hummocks.

Some lay down chewing their cud, others nursed fawns. Now and then a cow would lower her head and butt a yearling who had approached too close to her fawn. We drew near enough to hear the almost constant snorting and then, suddenly, they took fright and running with the motion of jointed puppets, stampeded across the frozen lake.

We stood and gazed after them in disgust. Surely we had approached as gently as possible.

Again, we started our stalking, having decided that Alec would encircle them on the right, I on the left, and Fred block them off at the rear. Elmer had told us it wasn't necessary to crouch when stalking—to walk upright, but deliberately, and to make no sudden movements. Still, as I came closer and closer, I thought my chances better if they took me for another reindeer and dropped to my knees. It did no good. Before they were in camera range, they stampeded back to where they had come from.

Not wishing to frighten them with our voices, we agreed by hand signals to repeat the maneuver and started out for the third time. Though we saw no signs of it, they had evidently agreed to repeat their response to our stalking and promptly stampeded away from us again. That was, except for one lone fawn whose mother turned and came back to hover over it, grunting "ow," "ow," while Fred photographed the pair from only a few feet away.

Alec, meanwhile, tried to head the herd back toward me but instead of falling in with his plan when they stampeded, they went directly back where they had been in the beginning.

I decided they might possibly repeat the cycle and hid beneath the bank of the lake ready for their next charge across. While I crouched and waited with cameras cocked, for some inexplicable reason, they allowed Fred to inch close enough to make the trip a photographic success. By using logic, I came off without a single shot, for though they stampeded in every direction around the lake, they never once crossed it the rest of the day.

Alec who had gone every step of the way with us plus some extra hunting, decided that night after supper he had been away from his family long enough and, hitching up our big team, took off in the greenish amber light of two hours before midnight. Lynx started out running with the team but with his tugline free.

The next day we packed up and started for the village

since we didn't want to take any chances on the ice breaking up and going out while we were away. We had smooth, fast going outside the inshore pressure ice though we had to go through sheets of water as deep as the basket of the sled.

Occasionally there were large holes in the ice—dark pools with bubbles rising in them. We watched anxiously for them for we knew of people losing their lives to the ice in spring. Elizabeth's father and his team drawing a sled with her mother holding an infant had all been lost in such a way. To our relief, Seegoo displayed an uncanny knowledge of the danger and even though he went through shallow water, carefully avoided the holes. We worried, too, whether or not Alec had made it safely home and upon arrival in the village went by his home to check. We were reassured to see his boots on the clothesline and the fresh seal skin nailed to the side of his house, showing he had met luck in the early morning hours.

A neighboring boy waved with the wing of a goose he was holding, then continued to make flying and gliding movements with it while his little sisters shot at him with sticks of wood.

As we neared Mik-nik-rok, we heard the sound of a motor and saw Gene testing his outboard in a barrel of water and then we saw a familiar figure coming towards us.

"Harold! We thought you had gone to Anchorage," Fred exclaimed.

"My emergency been put off," he told us. "T.B. cases sent first. I go next week."

"Is there any chance of your working with us for a few days?"

"Don't see why not," Harold replied. "Exercise won't hurt me. Just the cold."

"Can you go out with us tomorrow?"

"Sure."

That was all we needed. That and good weather and this time the weather came over to our side—with bright sun and flawless skies the next morning.

We obtained permission for Howard to leave school to go along and with Harold driving the big team and us the puppies, went back to the inshore pressure ice which had caused us so much trouble on the way to Egavik.

Our strategy was to shoot as many close-ups as was possible of Harold doing everything he was supposed to do in the final sequence. We "shot" him from every angle with several different exposures from early morning until the last direct ray of sunshine. We did the same thing the next day and for the three days after that.

On one of these days, Harold wanted to go fight a fire back of Unalakleet. We retained him by more than meeting the twenty-five dollars he would have been paid. Another day, he felt he should get ice to tide his wife over break-up. We hired someone else to do it. Relieved of these distractions, Harold was happy and cooperative. Going out with us gave him a chance to shoot at seals sunning on the ice and ducks and geese now flying north en masse.

We took extra appetizing, nourishing lunches and in addition, had Howard to breakfast and supper, so Howard was happy, too.

And when we had all the close-ups that would be needed for the finish of our movie "in the can," we were extremely happy.

There was even a day for Harold to go on a picnic with his family out on the tundra, and when or whether he left now made no difference in our movie plans, for Pete Kotongan had agreed to work with us.

All that held us up was the ice and it was—as it had been all along, an abiding worry.

At times, it appeared to be an almost solid sheet of water.

The river ice was covered with water, too, and separated from the banks by several feet. It was ready to break up. Surely, we thought, the pressure of the outpouring of ice would open a lead in the now rotten icefield, but it didn't.

When break-up came, there was no pressure at all, most of the ice having melted upriver. What was left just oozed out, chewing an opening of perhaps an eighth-mile at the rivermouth but beyond and around that, the field remained solid.

Instead of being a spectacular, incontestable division between winter and summer, it was nothing more than a gradual and inconclusive disappearance of river ice. Such an unheard of break-up was hardly a joyous event, marking liberation from winter's tyranny and the change from sleds to boats.

True, from then on we began to get our water upriver by outboard, first in the ice along the banks and then from the river after it had cleared. We brought water for the dogs down too, there being no drifts left around the cabin, our experiment of melting snow for dog water had come to an end. So far as we could determine, none of our dogs had suffered any ill effects and the time we saved in not getting extra ice was considerable.

We became convinced the sea ice was not going to break up and that we were not going to get a climax and without a climax we might just as well not have made the movie.

And then it happened—on a cold, rainy, foggy morning.

We looked out our west window and there—not a quarter mile away, was a blue line in the icefield. It was open water between the shorebound part of the field and the ice over deeper water.

We rushed out in a frenzy of excitement and climbed up on our roof with our binoculars for a better look. The lead extended along the coast as far as we could see. We hugged and pounded each other and jumped up and down and breathed deeply the first breath of air over salt water we had had since the fall before. Then, we began to sober up.

The icefield had broken, yes, but there could be no movies in the overcast for we had shot our close-ups of Harold in bright sunshine and our long and medium shots would have to tie in with them in lighting.

Now the waiting became more agonizing for, with the field broken, it went out and came back with the tides and wind and there was always the chance of its not returning at all.

Day after gloomy day, we watched and our spirits shuttled between despair and hope depending upon whether the ice was inshore or out to sea.

Even in this period of no sunshine and chilling fog, the villagers somehow knew to do the things that were always done in summer.

Thora who came in with the fur boots for us to send to the "store mans" outside, talked of going to hunt birds' eggs.

"Snipe eggs good," she said. "Gulls eggs good too and big —green with brown specks. White never get hard when cooked—just creamy. Muir eggs and crane eggs never even get creamy."

"Do they taste like hen eggs?" I asked.

Thora shook her head. "Naga. Taste like bird they come from."

The Russells left for their summer vacation.

Elizabeth, who was free now that her self-invited guest had become pregnant and left the village, went to gather wild rhubarb. It had the appearance of stalks of young onions but the taste of fresh apples.

Then, one morning, we looked out to find the fog and rain burned away by blinding, bright sunshine but the ice—the ice was so far out, it was only a thin white line against the horizon. Even with it that far out, we would have gone in pursuit had not an east wind been blowing and no one—not even the natives—went out on the ice then.

After that one day the west wind, fog and rain took over again.

Alec set buoys marking the now open river channel for the arrival of the first boat.

Little tots came knocking at the door holding strangled bouquets of flowers and grinning irresistibly. Our conversations ran something like this.

"Oh, you've been picking flowers?"

Nods and giggles and shuffling of feet. Sometimes stocking caps pulled down over faces in embarrassment.

"For whom did you pick them?"

More giggles.

"Did you pick them for your Mama?"

Head shakes.

Then I would name off the entire family.

More head shakes.

If they did not get up the nerve to say "for you," neither did I get up the nerve to ask directly. So I passed around the gum and marshmallows, the flowers were handed to me and out they trouped.

Men began leaving the village in company planes to work in the canneries.

Martha brought over the first king salmon.

Howard reminded us we had promised to take him on a picnic.

We decided as long as we couldn't be out on the ice, it would be as good a time as any to go.

We decided further that Seegoo and the puppies should be included in the fun since they had served us so faithfully.

We asked Choreboy Number eight, Eddie Kayoukluk, to go along to help because we were going in the boat—upriver to where the forests began.

Eddie would enjoy the boat ride and Howard a chance to climb trees. We ourselves would relish being in timber once more and there would be no problem of firewood or staking out the dogs.

We planned on being gone perhaps three hours and at the last moment, even though it was overcast, we found ourselves incapable of leaving our cameras.

On the morning of the picnic, the dogs lay sprawled around their houses resigned to a season of no snow and boredom, but when we brought the harnesses out, Seegoo sprang to life as did all the others.

They barked wildly and curtsied, raced around their posts, jumped on their houses and back down again and generally put on a great show of enthusiasm. Still, Fred and I suspected they were "showing off" for none of them barked with real conviction and several times, in the middle of all the excitement, one would stop to stretch and yawn or to scratch at the down they were beginning to shed.

Nanny and Newcah we harnessed at the rear of the sled since they were just coming out of their breeding period and Seegoo at lead with Sookgah and Kinguk just behind him. To prevent any harnesses getting tangled, Fred ran beside Seegoo and Eddie and Howard flanked the male puppies.

I was at the rear of the sled riding the brake for even though the sled was heavily loaded with an outboard motor, and grating over bare ground, the team went at a full gallop.

All went well until we reached the slough but once there, one complication followed another.

To keep Seegoo and the two make puppies from the two attractive females, I put myself between them in the bow of the boat, and the rest of the team. This, however, did not prevent communication in long-drawnout lovesick howls.

Eddie was in the stern with the two belles who were answering each mournful call with equally throbbing wails. Howard sat in the middle with the three constantly yapping sisters.

Fred stayed ashore and was setting up his cameras when, all at once, our boat came loose from its mooring and started drifting down the slough. I grabbed up a paddle but quickly tossed it to Howard for the moment I slackened a hold on any of the three males, they started towards the rear of the boat.

Howard let go of the chains of his three charges and manfully plunged the paddle into the water. The puppies immediately sprang to the sides of the boat and standing erect, forepaws braced against the frame, barked their contempt at everything and everybody in the passing landscape. Then, one of them started over the side.

"Howard," I yelled, "get the puppy."

Howard looked up, grabbed a furry hind leg and—dropped the paddle.

Eddie sprang to help and as he did, both of his puppies crawled up and over and splashed into the dark waters of the slough. Eddie leaped back, upended himself and by reaching out as far as he could, caught both pups by the scruff of the neck and began hauling them aboard.

Thus we made our way in wide circles down the slough while the villagers looked up from their cleaning of herring in utmost wonderment.

Fred, meanwhile, with cameras held high, leaped around the boats and over anchors and empty oil drums, as through an obstacle course and yelled to us to do something, we couldn't hear what.

At last, by taking a running jump from a boat we drifted

near to, Fred was able to get aboard. Then, for the first time in all the months we had used it—the spring, summer and fall before—the motor wouldn't start. While he turned knobs and made adjustments, not without audible comment, we continued on down toward the mouth of the river. When we reached the open sea, Fred gave up, grabbed a paddle and guided us to the flats on the opposite side.

"Now," Fred announced, "we will take the motor ashore and find out what's wrong with it."

Howard and I decided we might as well chain the dogs out and explore the flats while we waited.

I took Seegoo out first and chained him securely to a log of driftwood, then Kinguk and Sookgah. As Howard and I took the other sisters out, the rear end of the boat began easing away from the bank. Eddie who had one foot on the bank and one on the boat was pulled apart like a wishbone. Worse yet, he was holding the motor. Fred, standing in mud above the knees of his waders, tried to get to him but couldn't extricate himself in time. Eddie snapped his legs together and went in mud over his hip boots. The motor was completely buried. After digging it out, Fred decided we would have our picnic on the flats.

"We going to have our picnic *here?*" Howard asked, studying the treeless tundra.

"Yes," I told him. "It's getting late and we're all hungry. Don't you want to eat soon?"

The flats were all right with Howard.

While Seegoo and Sookgah and Kinguk warbled to Nanny and Newcah, we gathered driftwood for a fire and after what seemed a maximum effort coaxed a minimum flame from it. We filled a coffee can with water from one of the many ponds, then we hung it by its improvised wire handle on a forked stick we had slanted over the fire. Howard jabbed reindeer ribs like a picket fence around the flames and Eddie took off his boots to dry his pants. Things were looking up when—it began to rain and a cold wind came up from the east.

Not having anything to construct a lean-to, we crawled under a tarpaulin and waited. A wild ruckus among the dogs, however, forced Fred to go out to find Sookgah had chewed his towline in two and was cavorting with the girls. Fred repaired the damage and crawled back under the tarp.

The rain stopped, having gone on just long enough to put out our fire. Again we brought the wood to reluctant flame, so reluctant, it was late afternoon before the coffee came to a boil.

Fred set up the cameras to record our happy outing.

I poured out cups of steaming coffee, saw Eddie take a gulp, gag and spit it out. I tried it and gagged too. It was a concentrate of salt. We had not thought of it at the time, but the tundra pond from which we had drawn our water had been covered by high tides of the fall before.

Fred sighed. "We'll try another take. Don't drink any, just pretend to."

We pretended to drink and enjoy it and on this run, the camera jammed, breaking the film. Something had gone wrong with the mechanism. We loaded a stand-by camera and did retakes.

We could and did eat the ribs and as a special treat the oranges flown in from Anchorage. Before we finished eating, Fred went down to work on the motor only to find the boat beached in cementlike mud by the falling tide.

Howard, Eddie, all of us had to pull and push and strain to lift it free until we were plastered with mud from head to foot. Then, slogging through the sludge, we hand-lined it up the slough since the motor would not even turn over.

We went for the dogs—females first—and each in turn

splattered more mud on us as they wallowed from bank to boat and jumped in.

One at a time, we went for Seegoo, Sook and Kinguk who were so anxious to get to the boat, it took two of us to hold them.

Again across the slough—this time paddling—and into the sludge on the other side. Again the harnessing and the jolting, grinding, stampede across the spit.

As we unharnessed them, the rain started coming down. We came into the cold, dark cabin almost seven hours after leaving it and sank down—exhausted, wet, hungry, caked with mud. Our outboard motor was out of commission for we didn't know how long. One camera, though not our main one, was inoperative.

Outside, Seegoo continued his frustrated warbling to Nanny and Newcah. Through our west window, the sky was leaden, the drizzle a gray ectoplasm—the emanation of our hopes.

There was no icefield anywhere—not even far out.

"The movie isn't finished," Fred said wearily, "but it looks as if we are."

CHAPTER

16

The next day the ice was back within three miles off shore but the overcast and rain continued. The hunters who had been going out told us the floes were getting dangerously rotten and that they would surely break up if the field did not go out to sea for the final time soon.

The third day after our picnic the weather was overcast but as the morning went on we thought we could see a gradual lightening of the sky. This, plus the fact the ice seemed to be stationary at about four miles, was enough to cause us to develop a galloping case of hope again.

"I think I'll get Pete and Howard to be ready just in case it clears up," Fred decided.

While I prepared food and packed equipment, he alerted our crew. He also went to get the kayak we had rented—the only one of skin in the village—and hauled it on its sled down to the boat. By eleven o'clock we could restrain ourselves no longer and elected to go out just on the chance the sun would break through.

Again, we harnessed the pups and Seegoo, crossed the spit and, once at the slough, distributed them in the boat as before. This time we were using a larger boat, for in addition to the four of us and the eight dogs, we had to transport the sled, kayak and kayak sled.

Fred stood in the bow, behind him the kayak on its sled and our dog sled crossways to the boat, Pete manned the motor and Howard and I and all the dogs sat in the middle.

The puppies milled around completely unconcerned or stood on their hind legs staring down the villagers who stared at us as we zoomed down the slough into the open Bering Sea. We had no "belles" with us that day and so no frustrated serenading and no leaping into the water.

Pete followed the directions shouted by Fred until he felt we were in deep water, then he gave the motor full throttle.

We began to near an ice floe when suddenly there was a terrifying crash and the boat lurched so violently, Fred was almost thrown over the bow. None of us had to be told we had hit submerged ice. I reached across the cowering pups and unfastened the hook attaching Seegoo to the towline, for I expected the bottom of the boat to go out and all of us to have to swim for it.

Fred and I looked at each other, saw we were thinking the same thing and so said nothing. Pete said nothing.

Even the dogs ceased their shuffling and froze. Then, as the boat held and remained watertight, the awful moment passed.

I refastened Seegoo, Fred looked ahead again, the puppies came to life and Pete restarted the motor. The only effect of our collision was to lighten Pete's hand on the throttle from then on.

When we came to the first floe, we followed it around until we found a thick edge to pull alongside. Fred jumped out.

"How is it?" I called.

"No good. I don't think it will do." He returned to the boat. "There isn't even enough sound ice to harness the team on."

We went on to another floe and another. None were good enough to put a team on. Finally we found a floe with a lead going through it and here, in desperation, Fred took some shots of Howard and Pete though the light wasn't what he wanted. Before we could even finish this sequence, a wind started coming up and we had to hastily pack and head for shore. All of us were of the same mind—that the boat was tippy enough without a choppy sea beneath us.

Going back, we had to admit our first photographic effort on the ice field was a failure and whether or not we would have another chance we did not know. The weather was turning overcast and the cold wind hitting our faces was a wind from the east that might take the ice out for good. Added to that was the knowledge of just how rotten the ice was and even if the field stayed within range, there was no assurance we could find a usable floe. Again, our discouragement was complete.

The next day started as the one before, overcast with a promise of clearing. We concluded that while our chances were no better, neither were they worse, and so we should try again.

This time we paid Alec to go along and divided the load between us. With him went the kayak on its sled and the dog sled and in our larger boat rode Pete, Howard, myself and all the dogs with Fred at the motor.

We estimated the ice to be around seven miles out and so he headed straight to sea.

There was no wind and only slight swells and once we were at the field, the water was perfectly smooth. We wound among the floes looking for solid ice but with no luck.

Finally, Alec, who had come up close behind us and was standing up to look around, pointed to our left.

"How about over there?"

Fred nodded.

While Pete jumped out and pulled at the bow, Fred gunned the motor running the boat up on the ice enough to anchor it. Then he and Alec went to inspect the floe but what they found proved unsatisfactory for, from a distance, I saw Fred shake his head.

As they turned back, Alec glanced toward us with a start and said something. At the same moment, they began running.

"What's wrong?" I called.

"Get going," Alec yelled back, "the ice is jamming."

I looked back and saw a huge floe—one that had been a quarter of a mile away when we had stopped—now bearing down on us. Even as I watched, it came closer and seemed to gather momentum.

Pete had the motor going when Fred raced up and pushed us off and we started through the narrowing lead, Alec right behind. We did not care to think what would happen to our boat if the floes came together. Or, if we were adrift on rotten ice.

Unconsciously, Pete, Howard and I strained forward to help our boat get through. We came to the last few feet of the lead and felt a bump and then another. We were hitting a submerged shelf of ice that ran around the edge of the floe. Still, we were able to go forward although it was more like going over rough terrain than through water. At almost the exact moment we bumped our way into open water, Alec right after us, the floes came together with a thunderous impact. There followed the explosive sounds of gunfire as the ice split with new cracks, while a foot high ridge of pressure ice churned into being as the edges ground together.

Immediately we were caught in a backwash that set our boats to rocking and bobbing up and down. If we had been two boat-lengths back, or Alec one, we would never have made open water. We recalled with new understanding a saying we had heard many times, "Eskimo heart beats differently out on the ice."

We continued our search for sound ice and while we did, the last of the haze evaporated and the sun came out in full force.

It scatter-planted the sea with sparkling sequins and turned the icefloes into huge floating, luminous gems reflecting every shade of blue. There was the greenish opaque blue of the old pressure ice, the fresh, vibrant, transparent blue of new ice, the bluish purple of the cracks and the sapphire gleam of surface water. In this jewel-like setting, we, at last, found the exact location for which we had so long waited and searched.

There was a floe solid enough to sustain a team for a short distance and across a sixty foot lead (which was almost the exact width we required) another fairly solid floe.

As we set up our cameras, it was with a feeling fate was making a last, grand, conciliatory gesture towards us. If we failed to take advantage of it, there would be no more.

Fred looked at me. "This is it," he said. "Make or break."

I raised both hands and crossed my fingers. Then, we set to work.

The shooting script called for Pete, the father, to be caught on an ice floe while scouting for seal on foot, ahead of his dog team. His dog team, returning driverless to camp, alerted Howard, the son, to the situation. The son then set out with the team of puppies he had been training all year, only to find his father's kayak at the edge of the ice and his father adrift on a floe sixty feet away. The father solved the dilemma by throwing his ithlok (a wooden mallet equipped with deadly steel hooks for snaring seal) across the lead. The son, in turn, attached the rope of the ithlok to the kayak so it could be pulled across the open water and a rescue affected. The puppy, Sookgah, was the real hero, having brought the son to where the father was stranded. The rescue sequence was a test of Sooky, too. For the scene, he would have to lead the puppies alone, picking his way across treacherous ice to the place where Howard directed him.

We were set up.

Seegoo, who had been brought along to lead if we had struck out across a floe, was tethered to an ice bridge—a wicket chiseled in the floe.

Pete stood at the edge of the ice across the lead, ready to wave to his son. Fred was immediately behind him with the camera covering both Pete and Howard's approach. Alec had Sookgah by the collar, for Howard by himself could not hold the puppy team back and I was covering the approach from a different angle some distance away from the lead.

This was the moment.

For this, we had brought the puppies through the winter. Upon this, the finish of our movie depended. Would Sookgah live up to the tradition of his breed?

Fred gave the signal. Alec released Sookgah and Howard shouted "Gih."

Sookgah catapulted forward. Behind him the team sprang to action. On they came, Sookgah setting a pace to keep a taut towline. It was a thrilling sight—the puppies all running in unison, beautifully conformed, tails aplume and matched in pairs behind Sookgah. And Sookgah—showier than ever with an extra lift to his gait, a proud angle to his head, self assured—had come into his own.

There was an anguished cry from Seegoo when he realized the puppy was taking over his place as leader, but Sookgah took no notice. Forward he went until Howard called "whoa" at the place on the edge of the ice opposite Pete. Then he stopped to look questioningly at his master for he wanted very much to go on. Once assured that he was to stay, he turned to survey the rest of the team with just the touch of majesty his father possessed.

Pete threw the ithlok, Howard went through his part of the business, the father reached safety, embraced his son who in turn hugged the puppy leader. Both Howard and Pete did inspired jobs, getting into the spirit, feeling the story to the point where we, ourselves, were moved. Then, the same thing again and again, each time with different exposure.

With the third run completed, Fred and Pete prepared to come over to our side for the necessary medium shots. By then, I was back with Seegoo. I remember I looked and saw Pete carefully picking his way toward the lead with his niksik (ice pick). Fred set the camera down and started for its case and suddenly I was just seeing one man—Pete. The camera still stood, but Fred was gone.

Completely disappeared through the ice.

I started screaming and running.

"Pete! Pete! Get him! Get him!"

Pete wheeled, saw what had happened and with a look of terrible anxiety, started racing back to where Fred had been.

Alec was running after me, shouting, "Sara, don't jump in the water. I'll get the boat. Wait!"

On the other side, Fred's head bobbed out of the water in a large hole in the ice.

He was trying to crawl out but the undercut rotten edge kept breaking off. He was weighted down, his hip boots filled with water, his fur parka soaked. In desperation, he started flailing at the edge of the opening with his elbows.

We all knew life in sub-arctic waters was counted in seconds, or that at any instant, the swift current could sweep him under the ice. And *I* knew I could never reach him in time.

I came to the lead and Alec grabbed me.

"Wait. We go in boat." Not releasing my arm he brought the boat to with his free hand. Then he stopped.

Fred had heaved himself out of the water as far as his waist when Pete reached him and grabbing the nape of his parka hauled him out like a puppy. All in the same movement, Fred rolled over on his back and Pete pulled off his boots, the water gushing out. Then, as Fred sat up, Pete peeled off his soaked parka.

I sagged against the boat.

"It's all right." Alec's voice was reassuring, still I could not find the strength to stand.

Fred wrung out his socks, put his boots back on, climbed into the boat with Pete and they started across.

Alec, who had been tactfully standing off a bit, came over to me.

"You O.K. now?"

"Yes."

"You gave me a scare. I thought you were going to jump."

"I don't know what I was to do, Alec."

The boat came alongside and Fred hurried over. We looked at each other. We did not smile. It had been too close to get over that quickly. We did not speak. There was no need. After some seconds, Fred pressed my shoulder and went to the boat.

"We going in?" Howard asked.

Fred was putting on a spare jacket. "Not as long as there's sunshine, my boy," he used the tone they always joked with.

"Well, what now?" I had found my voice.

"The same thing all over again for medium and close-ups." Having at last come into sunshine, Fred was making the most of it.

Several more times we went through the same action for medium shots and each time Sookgah performed like a veteran. As I watched him, I knew we could never leave the gallant, lovable puppy behind—that we would take him along with Seegoo when we went.

We started on our close-ups. By then it was late afternoon and though the sun was still high in the skies, a freshening wind put a chill in the air and roughened the water. I noticed Fred beginning to stamp up and down and flex his arms to get warm, but still there was no mention of going in.

He had just picked up his camera and was backing away to study another angle when it happened again.

The ice beneath him gave way like a trap door.

I saw the look of surprise on his face, then automatically, he shoved the camera above his head—a useless gesture for he plunged so hard, it went under too. I was the nearest and first to get to him. He was desperately treading water to stay afloat and holding the camera above his head. I reached for the scruff of his parka as Pete had done.

"No, no," he yelled. "Take the camera."

I did as he said. "Grab the tripod. I'll pull you out."

"No—I'm all right. Take the camera."

With that ultimate self-abnegation for the movie, my anger boiled up and over.

"Damn the camera." I slammed it and the tripod down

on the sled and turning gave my husband a yank which pulled him not only out of the water but well onto the ice. "*Now* we go in." I blazed.

"All right," he answered mildly enough to take me by surprise, but I shouldn't have been. The climax of the movie was "in the can" and Fred probably surmised that our cinemascope lens was ruined, which it was (by its dunking rather than my violence) though the film came through undamaged.

Alec, who had been watching from a distance, decided my equanimity had been restored.

"Well, the camera was the last thing under and the first thing out," he said grinning as he came up.

The tension broken, we hurriedly packed to leave. The wind was now producing long swells in the water and we could feel the floe undulating beneath us. We felt them on the ride back holding us back and then on the crest, giving us a downhill push.

Fred was miserably cold but had it been necessary he would without any doubt have taken the two dunkings all over again, for it meant a year's work. Seegoo sat next to him providing warmth. Gentle, faithful Seegoo. We had decided if he came through for us this year, he could take it easy for the rest of his life. He had more than earned an untrammeled retirement.

We approached the village—mellowed by the gold of the late afternoon sun. The spit was flat again. Where once were drifts, now grew the deep, green grass.

We entered the slough and pulled into shore and as we cut our motors, I was struck by the absolute quiet of the village.

Fred jumped out to hurry ahead and build a fire and change clothes, while Alec and Pete harnessed the dogs and started off with them to the cabin. Their progress was marked by spates of lethargic barks from spectator dogs, but from only a few. Mostly they remained stretched to their full length in the grass and didn't bother to open their eyes.

I walked alone across the spit. Up the main path I saw a friend and called out to her. My voice hung in the air. Not until she was close did she violate the hush with a soft-voiced greeting.

Then, past the house where Sarah lived—gone with her family trapping for squirrels. Sarah, who had asked before she left, "Where you go when you leave?"

"Outside and after that to our home in Matanuska Valley."

"Will you ever come back to Unalakleet?" she wanted to know.

"Maybe. Sometime."

"When you come back, can I be your dishwasher?"

I assured her she could.

"No matter when?"

I said yes. . . .

Past Thora's house. The "mans" at the store outside had liked the boots, but no more orders came for they had been too long in delivery. Even had there been orders, Thora was much too busy to be a "boss womans." Now, she was gone hunting eggs.

Past Elizabeth's house—out gathering more greens.

Past other houses standing empty for the summer while families went camping. Back to the forests along the river filled with fish for themselves and for their dogs.

It was the carefree time. Old problems forgotten. No one agitating for Unalakleet to change from reservation to city. No one cared.

For a time the lives of the villagers would be relaxed, leisurely. Their living no longer revolved around the getting of wood and water—and the howl of the Malemute.

And suddenly, and with a sharp sense of loss, I realized —neither did ours.